Praise for

My Life's a Mess – But I Can Fix It!

"I'm a clinical hypnotherapist and as I studied the example of what a new life blueprint might look like in the excellent book "My Life's a Mess – But I Can Fix It! " by Andrea Lucas, I got "goose bumps"! Over the years I have learned that this is Spirit's way of telling me, "this is good stuff". This book is a wonderful "behind the scenes" look into the private life of an extraordinary woman, and proves yet again that you CAN shape or reshape your life any way you want!

The explanations and examples are easy to follow and will help you understand what makes you tick, and the step by step instructions will show you how to reinvent your personal blueprint and fulfill your life's desire. Don't know what that is? She'll help you figure that out too! This book will be required reading for my all my clients."

Doug Ottersberg
Change Agent, NM

~

"Andrea Lucas' book is a beautiful reminder from someone who has been there that we can all improve our outlook on life once we have identified what keeps us tethered to the lead balloons from our past. It is easy to read, offers encouragement on every page, and best of all, contains concrete instructions for exercises that really work. Everyone can try them – they certainly work for me!"

Brigitte Strelka, NY

~

"What a great metaphor for restructuring a life by getting down to the basic plans and designs for living."

Tom Foley, Oregon

~

"I like your book and will recommend it. Strengthening the American character is critical ... I believe you help guide the way."

Sidney T. Rimmington, CA

"The way you have related your own life experiences in regard to our "blueprints" is very powerful and triggers memories for me some of which feel good and some which feel "not so good". But I understand that in the big picture of things it is about experience on the earth plane and not about our judgments of it! I am one of those souls who had to hit rock bottom more than once in order to start paying attention to my thoughts and conditioning. You have indeed served a vital part of my path to self discovery and actualization and it is always wonderful to hear things presented in different ways. Thank you for sharing your life experiences!"

Namaste

Richard S., Canada

"I started tearing up while reading the first pages. I have a feeling that your book is going to change my life because already it has touched some very deep places. And, like you, I have repressed so much just so I can get on with life, sort of. Thank you for the book."

Carol DeLis, AZ

"I am glad to have read your book – your wise logic and argumentation that is understandable by all brought me cosmic joy!"

Dr. Tibor Nagypal, Vienna, Austria

"I surprised myself when halfway through your book I found that I had indeed been inspired to look deeper and closer into my inner self and begun to reflect on the many steps that had forged the person I am today; the many experiences that have impacted and created my persona (my personality). This awakening was in some respects not always a very pleasant experience but a few days later I find that I can better understand why I am what I am, why I do what I do; why I feel what I feel and why I still desperately seek fulfillment after a lifetime of what many might deem to have already been a bucket-full of successes. I daresay your self-revealing book will impact your readers in different manners; but in my case, it has proven to be well worth the investment in time and effort. I am hopeful that others shall similarly find their true selves and then be able to build on that foundation the new identity they really wish to achieve. Thanks and best wishes,"

A.I.D.Francis, P.R.

"I know a lot of what you have put into this book, already, thanks to classes, reading, talking with many people, and reading so many self-help books. Yet I think you have done a very good job of pulling it all together! Being able to illustrate and use your life for examples makes it a wonderful Blueprint for others to use!"

John Kubik, CA

❧

"Your writing style is so natural, fluid and vivid. The information is clear, the stories are very much alive and optimistic. Excellent Book Writing. What I found most interesting is how well you described the obvious yet unnoticed forces influencing our lives moment by moment. To paint the picture of past experiences with the emotions and put them into a framework and then correlate them to the Laws of Cause and Effect was absolutely brilliant insight. Your book will help raise the consciousness of everyday people. It will inspire others to review who they have become, trace the cause, and choose to create who they want to be in the future. How Great is that? This is what free will is all about. Loved the book. Looking forward to really delving into the exercises!"

Patricia Shelton, VA

❧

"Andrea Lucas is one of those rare individuals whose life and accomplishments sound too good to be true. Yet her life is very real. Her amazing experiences are tempered by a down to earth personality and rich compassion for others. She has achieved incredible success and overcome many obstacles. She can help you do the same. Andrea is an incredible woman with stories to tell and more important, wisdom to share. Listen to her and grow."

Jason E Borton
Abundance Educator

❧

"I can't get enough of Andrea. She communicates strength and clarity. I feel inspired by her and her words are so truthful."

Sylvia Ryker, CA

❧

"Andrea's book is phenomenal! She speaks to your heart and reveals simple, yet profound secrets to happiness, prosperity and fulfillment in every aspect of your life. I am very fortunate to be Andrea's close friend and to have witnessed such powerful changes in her life since she discovered her Script. Open your heart to be touched by Andrea's love and wisdom and your life will change forever."

Olga Jegaline
Kelowna, Canada

⌒

"I laughed and I cried… Andrea Lucas' book is profoundly enlightening and life transformational! Through her captivating storytelling she shines a 1000 watt spotlight on the readers' life, unmasking hidden "blueprints" for love, money and health which allow you to radically change your life and fill it with joy, happiness and abundance!"

Joe Rickards
Vancouver, Canada

⌒

A Powerful Book

"Andrea is living proof of the potential of every human being. Our early experiences shape our lives and the understanding and awareness of them then gives us the power to live the life we love. Enjoy the journey."

Vincent Pizzitola, FL

⌒

"Andrea is an amazing woman that I've had the pleasure to get to know through my own journey of enlightenment. We all have our own Scripts or baggage that we have to deal with. I'm sure Andrea can help you shorten or make easier your own journey if you listen and take to heart what she has to say."

Eberhard Samlowski, CA

⌒

"I think the best type of instructor is the one who has lived through the process. I've seen Andrea completely change her life, crack her old script and create a new destiny. She is a delight and truly a gift. I've seen her go from protected and withdrawn to alive and light by using the exact tools taught in her book. Andrea is someone who has lived the work. Also, she's someone who is living proof that money, success and fame don't make happiness, peace nor contentment – intentional self-creation by processes like the methods described in this book do."

Jase Souder
Founder, Life Tigers LLC

⌒

"Andrea Lucas has lived more and done more than anyone I know. Her book is filled with heart-breaking stories and amazing breakthroughs that will benefit anyone that reads it."

Darrell Wingerak, MI

⇌

"I read Andrea Lucas' book with great interest and benefit. Each page reflects the personal commitment with which the author approached her work. Using personal life experiences she explains the basic parameters of her book: when autobiographical scars develop into self fulfilling prophesies, they often define one's life path. The objective of the book is to show the way out of such a vicious cycle. After a brief introduction into the theory of the subconscious mind, finding the crucial points of one's Blueprint are discussed as well as the role of professional assistance during this process. The subsequent chapters are devoted to restructuring of this Blueprint with special emphasis on positive reinforcements. Of great benefit are the practical and simple to execute suggestions for visualization of goals and desires that bring results – after all, that's the difference between wishing and choosing!

Of further importance is the author's offer to give personal feedback to her readers. The simple to understand and convincing language of the author, that quickly evokes the reader's emotional concurrence adds significantly to the overall positive impression of the book. Persons who shy away from psychologists and psychotherapists because they fear being labeled "crazy" (which is still widely the case), will benefit greatly from this book. "My Life's a Mess - But I CAN Fix It!" can therefore be recommended as entry reading for all patients who are afraid to face their personal problems, let alone seek professional assistance."

Dr. Rembert Vollmer, Neurologist
Vienna, Austria (Translated from German)

⇌

"As an author myself I am always keen to see what the competition is up to. Andrea is in a class by herself and is a 'must-read'."

John Hollingsworth

⇌

"Andrea Lucas is, in a word, amazing. You owe it to yourself to go through her site, buy her book and get on with a life filled with purpose and joy. "

Glenn Dietzel
AwakenTheAuthorWithin.com

My Life's A Mess...

But I Can Fix It

Reprint Your Blueprint and Grow Happy & Rich!

Andrea R. Lucas

To my children, who have become

amazing adults in spite of their mother's blueprint.

Table of Contents

Foreword

Dear Reader,

This is a Happy Book - a book that is meant to inspire you to take charge of your life and change your old Blueprint if it no longer serves you. A Blueprint refers to the way in which you see the world and your place in it. It is usually formed in early childhood, most of the time through some traumatic event that has an enormous psychological impact on a child. The emotions triggered as a result of such trauma create a coping mechanism in the child's subconscious mind that becomes the Blueprint of how he will live his life.

When you read the Preface and the first chapter of this book you will encounter descriptions of traumatic events that might resonate with you negatively if you yourself were victim of similar events. Do not let this deter you from reading on – this book is not about childhood trauma. It is about showing you the way to conquer old demons and live a life full of fulfillment and happiness!

Andrea R Lucas

Preface

The child wakes up, startled by loud voices coming from the next room – Mutti's room (Mutti is the German word for Mommy). Someone is there, someone with a deep and angry voice – a man, she thinks, it must be a man. She can't make out the words, but she knows Mutti is there and Mutti is scared…and fear grips her little heart as she tries to make sense of what she hears. She is wide awake now. Silently she glides out from under the covers, lowers herself from the bed to the floor and crouches low so as not to be discovered and not to wake her brother and sister sleeping in the same room. It is dark and the door to Mutti's room is closed. Still, light is seeping through the opening in the wall behind the living room coal stove. Slowly the child inches to that place – her favorite hiding place in the world, and sinks onto the soft cushions next to Mausie, the family cat. She presses the little creature to her body for warmth and reassurance as she strains her eyes to see what's going on in the other room.

Terror grips her and her little body turns rigid as comprehension sinks in. There is Mutti sitting on a chair backed to the wall, her arms up in the air as she is trying to protect her face from the blows. She is crying and tears are streaming down her face. This man, this huge and ugly man is shouting and yelling, and hitting Mutti with his fists – wham! wham! – over and over again. Mutti is cowering, blood streaming from her swollen, unrecognizable face, her cries mere whimpers now – a door slams shut and then the room falls silent.

The little girl cries out – Mutti, Mutti, I'm coming, I'm coming, please don't cry, *please don't hurt so much, let's run away you and me, you can do it, I'll help you get away, Mutti, Mutti, I'm here to help you, I'll make it all better, you'll see, you'll see – but no sound passes from her terrified lips. She cannot move - it is as if a giant hand has pinned her down and squeezed out all the strength from her body. No matter how much she struggles in her mind to get away, to run to Mutti, to protect her, to comfort her, nothing she does makes a difference – the giant hand clenches her throat now, and she cannot breathe. Panic sets in and an unbearable belief forms in her trembling heart at that moment that will haunt her for the rest of her life. This belief evolves into a program designed to protect her, to erect walls and safeguard her and to keep out the dangerous world.*

⤳

The year was 1948 and the child was I at age 5; and this big and ugly man was my father, who hit my mother for one reason or another – or for no reason at all. I don't know. My father had been away at the war, stationed here and there, and was never at home, or infrequently enough that a five year old could not remember who he was when he showed up that day. In fact, I remember very little of him at all. That may be because over the years I have perfected the art of forgetting – pushing all unpleasant memories into the deep recesses of my mind.

I grew up in Vienna, Austria, right in the center of town, a stone's throw from the famous St. Stefan Cathedral. I was the middle of three children – not an enviable position as I found out during my youth and adolescent years. We were neither rich nor poor – just average middle class. Although our apartment had only two rooms, they were large enough to ride a bicycle around in them – which I tested of course on many occasions. Our bathroom and kitchen were combined in one room, which made for quick wash routines, and there was a separate toilet – inside the apartment, a luxury at that time. I shared the one room with my older sister and younger brother, and the other room was both the living room and our mother's bedroom. I do not remember our father ever living with us. I know that shortly after that night he left us for good – he went to Venezuela and landed in Brazil a few years later, where he remained the rest of his life.

I grew up fatherless and had no male role models in my life to speak of – no uncles or other relatives who could have taken his place. Yet something had happened that night of the "incident" as I have chosen to call the assault, that had already created an image in my mind of what men were all about – and no other role model was needed. You see, in the simplistic mind of a 5 year old, it was all quite clear:

➢ Men were strong and powerful

➢ Men were dominant, potent, commanding

➢ Men were controlling, they could do whatever they wanted

➢ Men were cruel and violent, they hit women, and

➢ Men were not to be trusted

And so for every image I had of a man, I also created an image of a woman, based solely on the reality I had witnessed that night:

➢ Women were weak, feeble, fragile

➢ Women were vulnerable, they could not defend themselves

➢ Women were inadequate, they were being taken advantage of by men

➢ Women were soft and delicate, but it was not safe to be a women if men could hurt them

➢ The world was not a safe place for women

Right from the start I knew that I was different – I was not going to be one of "the girls". I cannot remember ever having a doll, or playing with girl's toys or pretending to be "Mommy" when engaged in the typical child's play of family interactions. I cannot remember having friends. Of course, life was different in Austria then. There were no other children living in our apartment building, and the only place for play was in the public parks. We did not go there frequently because adults had to take us there and that was not often possible. Our mother worked, and Grandma was too old to make the trip every day. That left elementary school for interaction with other children, and I made my mark there early on…

Surely I was loved as a child, but I never knew it.

Surely I was loved as a child, but I never knew it. Showing affection was frowned on in our family. Our mother

19

presented to the world the image of a strong woman who bore her shame (of having been deserted by her husband) with her head high. She may have succeeded in fooling others, but she could not fool me. I knew in my heart that she was helpless. After the "incident" everything changed. I could not climb on my mother's lap and feel safe. I could not look at her and feel happy. I could not let her near me, for she personified danger…

I remember feeling ill one night. My mother was at my bedside, and she reached out to touch my forehead to check for fever. I shrank away from her, I could not let her touch me – it was like she would inflict some horrible disease on me, she would pass on to me the weakness, the feebleness and vulnerability of a woman. I did not want to be vulnerable.

I wanted to feel safe and secure. I wanted to be loved, and there was no one there to love me (the words "I love you" were never spoken in our house). And if nobody loved me, I must have been unlovable and thus unworthy of love.

Feeling unloved, unworthy and living in an unsafe world presented a real dilemma…

Feeling unloved, unworthy and living in an unsafe world presented a real dilemma and emotional trauma to me growing up. How could I grow up to be a woman and live in a woman's world where there is constant danger of being hurt? The recollection of my mother's pain and the terror I felt that night was too much to bear. With every breath I took the conviction drew nearer that there was really only one solution: choose the lesser of the two evils. "You cannot be vulnerable. You cannot allow yourself to become like your mother. You cannot live in fear. You must become strong and powerful yourself like a man, even though men are despicable. To survive in this world as a woman, you have to outfox, outsmart and outperform all male competitors, no matter what the arena. Only then will you stand a chance of making it and feeling safe…"

And thus unbeknownst to me, a script was formed, a blueprint through which my life, my outward personality was molded. As I grew older, subconsciously I embarked on my path of becoming strong and tough, eating more and gaining weight. I became feisty, muscular and fat and outweighed and outgrew all of my classmates. In high school I chose the kind of sports that would support my belief system. Fencing, judo, swimming and horseback riding were my favorite ones, all boys' sports of course. There were no ballet, gymnastics or baton twirling classes in my repertoire. I was called a tomboy, fatso, rebel and surely many other unpleasant names that I choose not to recollect.

I want to point out, though, that I never had gender orientation issues, nor did I end up hating men. I never saw myself as a man, had no need to "be" a man, I just saw myself living in a man's world and playing by men's rules. What's good for the goose is good for the gander – except that in my case it was the other way around: what's good for the gander is good for the goose.....

And all the while I was on the path of becoming the strong and powerful woman I wanted to be, there was the hidden fear, the conviction of my helplessness that was nagging and always present, ready to surface at just the most crucial moment. "You are a woman! You are helpless, you can't make a difference. Whom are you kidding? You can pretend to be strong and powerful like a man, but you know you can't pull it off. You cowered and froze when it counted the most, you could not help your mother then, what makes you think you can make a difference now? You'll always be weak, you are condemned to failure, you haven't got it in you to succeed in a man's world, you are a loser and you'll always be one!"

This battle was raging in me all my life. I could never be happy about my accomplishments, as the voices inside my head stirred up conflicting emotions. Self doubt robbed me of great joy and the feeling of personal fulfillment. My blueprint warped and mutated my view of the world. It was like I had put on a pair of tinted glasses that obscured my view, that painted every experience of my life with the conviction that men were cruel and not to be trusted and that women were weak and powerless.

And the terrible truth is, of course, that none of this is true. Men are not cruel, and women are not weak,

Blueprint for Andrea's Life

Henceforth I shall believe that...

I am incapable
I am unloved
I am worthless
I can't make a difference

Men are cruel
Men are powerful
Men cannot be trusted
Women are weak
Women are vulnerable

The world is harsh for women
The world is dangerous for women
The world is not safe
Life is not safe

The future is bleak
I'll never fit in
I'll never be able to make a difference
Nobody will love me

21

life is in fact safe! It was my own interpretation of the "incident" that led to the formation of my blueprint. I know this now – but I did not know this for the past 60 years. I was blessed to have been guided on a path of self discovery and self improvement recently, and only through this journey did I come to the understanding of my blueprint. It is said that "awareness is half the battle" – and so it is. Knowing about and understanding my blueprint has allowed me to look at my life in a totally new light. It has empowered me, it has made me realize that I was not the l failure I thought I was, that I have achieved many great things in my life.

I will reveal through the chapters of this book – using examples from my life – how my blueprint made me put myself down time after time, never allowing me to see what others saw. I was living my own legacy, I just did not know it.

∽

The events of childhood do not pass, but repeat themselves like seasons of the year.

Eleanor Farjeon

∽

Chapter 1

How Blueprints Are Formed

I want you to understand that everyone has an experience in their early childhood that influences their life somehow. Many psychologists say that blueprints are formed as early as at birth. Imagine the terror a newborn infant must feel when expulsed from the warm and safe cocoon of its mother's womb into the blindingly bright light and ice cold temperature of a hospital delivery room. If that infant is not immediately held and loved and reassured of its mother's love, a blueprint might be formed by that traumatic experience that says "she does not love me, I am worthless, I am alone in this harsh outside world, I don't want to be here" and this feeling of abandonment and worthlessness can stay with him or her throughout life.

During the first 9 months of a baby's life it needs to be held, nurtured and reassured constantly. Numerous studies have shown that when human touch is lacking in an infant's early childhood development, normal growth and development is stunted and a child can literally wither and die. I had a friend once, an older gentleman, who spent all his free time holding and rocking AIDS and crack babies who had been abandoned by their mothers. Hospitals across the nation have instituted such "rocking" programs to provide this vital support to newborns when nursing staff cannot provide it for lack of time.

A child is most susceptible between the ages of 3-7; these are the "growth" years during which a child is most malleable. And even if nothing out of the ordinary happens during those years, children learn by imitating the adults around them and thus habits are formed that have their roots in the words and actions of their parents, teachers and other adult role models.

What is a blueprint?

When I am speaking of a blueprint I really do have a blueprint in mind that is used for every construction job you can imagine. If you are building a house your blueprint could look something like this: it has drawings and calculations to ensure that the design is to

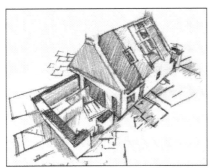

the liking of the customer and the materials used are strong enough to support the structure as envisioned by the architect.

But what if you are building a car? You'd still need a blueprint, only this time it defines the shape of the vehicle and the power of the engine, the interior comfort of the car, the materials used for the seats, the stereo and all other attributes. Without this blueprint you would not be able to tell the machine shop how to mold the metal frame into the shape of the car, nor the engine manufacturer how to cast the engine block, nor the factory mechanics how to put the entire car together.

When a child embarks on his or her journey of life, he also needs a blueprint. What kind of life is he creating for himself - a happy and fulfilled life or one of loneliness and despair? Will she be successful in whatever she undertakes or fail in every attempt? Will he see beauty in life, trust in his instincts and create a life full of wonder and accomplishment? What structures and building blocks will she use to build this wonderful life she dreams about?

A child of course cannot knowingly draw this blueprint for himself until he reaches adulthood. Nevertheless, the blueprint is formed by the impressions the child receives from the moment he has cognitive capability, which according to scientists is after the third month of conception. Yes, even while still in her mother's womb, the unborn child receives messages and interprets them. He forms impressions about the world he is going to be borne into. Is this a kind and benevolent world or a hostile and difficult one? Will she be loved and cared for?

These initial impressions are then confirmed or revised after birth based on the life experiences the child encounters. As indicated above, the incredible growth years of a child are between the ages of 3-7; so it is no wonder that any and all experiences a child has during those years have a profound impact on the child's outlook on life – on his or her blueprint.

The foundations for life are set during these years, and just like in a construction job, once the foundations are set in concrete, it is very challenging to change them. It is their job to be solid, to support the structures to be built on them. Life's foundations and blueprints are very hard to change – unless you know how, and this is what you are going to learn how to do in this book. Life blueprints are also called Scripts or Life-Scripts by some authors and psychiatrists.

Negative blueprints

There can be positive and negative blueprints. Unfortunately, all too many blueprints are negative. Here is an example of a negative blueprint that you may easily recognize:

Father and son are engaged in baseball practice; the little boy tries to hit the ball, but every time he swings the bat, swoosh, he hits nothing but air. He tries again, and again, and with every miss, his eagerness to please his Dad evaporates some more and fear creeps up. He is tired now, and glances at his Dad, whose facial expression has changed from tolerant to clearly upset and disappointed. The little boy starts crying, but Dad won't let go. His voice is sharp and elevated – "You are doing it wrong! How many times do I have to tell you how to hold the bat? Swing this way, not that way! You'll never be any good at this if you can't even get the basics right! You call this a swing? What's the matter with you? Are you stupid or something?"

The little boy is sobbing now, afraid to move, afraid to make another mistake to get his Dad even angrier. And then come the words that shall be forever remembered by the subconscious mind as daggers thrust into his heart and soul " I don't know why I bother with you! I should play with your brother instead – he pays attention when I say something – he's got the talent. You are just useless, useless, useless..."

This child will grow up hearing these damning words in his mind's voice over and over again. His opinion of himself will be poor, he'll have low self esteem and really believe that he is useless... Words can hurt more than any physical blow. A bruise of the flesh heals quickly and is often soon forgotten. A blow to the mind however has a devastating effect; once it's landed, it grows and festers, and encroaches on thoughts and feelings and won't stop until it has clearly imprinted itself on the mind....

Entertainers and famous people share their traumatic childhood experiences

It is not hard to find real life examples of negative blueprints. Many entertainers and famous people have come out recently to share with the world their traumatic childhood experiences. They did this because they knew that as entertainers their message will be heard by thousands if not millions of people who might have experienced similar traumas in their lives and who could be helped by knowing that they are not alone in their plight.

While we may not ever know the morbid details of how their negative blueprints were formed (unless immortalized by a movie like in "Walk The Line" - see below), all we have to do is read between the lines and imagine what it must have been like to be …

➤ Oprah: Oprah Winfrey lived with her grandparents after her parents separated when she was only six years old. She lived in very poor surroundings in a hostile environment where she was sexually molested by male relatives. She had to endure this hardship until 14, when she moved to live with her father. Oprah struggled with drugs, weight, and rebellious behavior and lost a baby after giving birth prematurely.

➤ Ben Kingsley: Ben Kingsley spoke at an interview about a character he was playing in "Sexy Beast": "I found him inside with little research at all. He is the darkest side of me that I had an opportunity to visit, and I've found him very empowering to play. My first step was to find the wounded child inside, and then all the subsequent steps fitted in after that. Don Logan (the character) is a man who is desperate to be loved, who is desperate to love, desperate to be needed, to have a role, to be seen and admired. And I think the wounded child inside him has turned into a screaming psychopath because those wounds have never been addressed."

➤ Charlize Theron: This beautiful actress from South Africa stunned the world with her performance as serial killer/prostitute Aileen Carol Wuornos in the film "Monster". She completely transformed her physical appearance into that of an ugly hooker and probably drew on the horrors of her own childhood trauma to portray her character's views about men and abuse. Charlize's father was abusing her mother regularly, who fought back one night and killed him. The shooting was called self defense and no charges were filed against her mother.

➤ Linda Hamilton, an actress well known for her roles in the Terminator series, the Beauty and the Beast, Dante's Peak and Point Last Seen, was diagnosed with bipolar disorder at an early age. Could it have been caused by the trauma of losing her father at age 5 when he was killed in an auto accident?

➤ Anne Heche, actress, opened up to Barbara Walters in an ABC Interview that sexual abuse by her father until she was 12 drove her "insane". "I had a fantasy world that I escaped to. I did a lot of things in my life to get away from what had happened to me" she said. "I drank, I smoked, I did drugs, I had sex ... I did anything to get the shame out of my life."

➤ Johnny Cash, musician and entertainer, whose life was chronicled in the 2006 movie "Walk The Line", struggled all his life to overcome damning words his father said to him when his brother died. This film depicts the early life of Johnny Cash and the exact moment when his blueprint was formed: after the accidental death of Johnny's older brother, his father blames Johnny – he grabs an empty tin can from a cupboard and yells at him "See this! See this – there's nothing! Nothing! And that's what you are! You are nothing! He (God) took the wrong son!"

➤ Roseanne, comedian and actress, announced publicly in 1994 that she had been diagnosed with multiple personality disorder, obsessive compulsive disorder, depression and agoraphobia. In her autobiography "My Lives" she reveals a childhood marked by sexual, physical and verbal abuse allegedly committed by her parents.

And the list goes on: there is Teri Hatcher, actress, who was molested frequently by her uncle; she says "These are haunting things that I've remembered all my life". There is talk show host Ricki Lake, who blames childhood sexual abuse for her weight issues;

there is Wynona Judd, country singer and songwriter, who suffered sexual abuse as a child and has struggled with emotional eating all her life.

Irish singer and songwriter Sinead O'Connor was physically, sexually and emotionally abused by her parents; her songs reflect her pain and suffering. And then there is actor Robert Blake, who also was physically, sexually and emotionally abused by his parents for many years. And sweetheart model and actress Sandra Dee was sexually abused by her stepfather at the age of 8; she struggled with eating disorders and had a drinking problem.

Every one of the famous people mentioned above ultimately became a success story. They had the inner strength to overcome the suffering of their horrible childhoods. They achieved this triumph, whether by themselves or with help from a counselor, priest, psychiatrist or a friend, it does not matter. What does matter is that they moved on...

Dean Koontz, suspense novelist, says in a recent article that, although he endured a torturous upbringing – extreme poverty and a frighteningly abusive, alcoholic father, "I don't think that I have great psychic scars. There were a lot of terrible things in my childhood, but I was also a pretty happy kid. I remember looking around at the world and seeing beauty almost everywhere..."

Not all negative blueprints stem from physical or sexual abuse. Negative blueprints are also formed by conditional love, when a child is told through spoken and unspoken words that he will only be loved if certain conditions are met: "If you are good, I will love you"; "If you clean up your room, I will love you"; and if the child has cleaned up his room a new condition is set, like: "If you take out the trash like I told you, I will love you"; and after that: "If you stop fighting with your brother, I will love you"; and so on.

Negative blueprints are also formed by conditional love...

The standards for achievement of a parent's love always escalate so that the child can never reach them.

In the mind of the child this translates to "No matter what I do, I can never do it right; I am a loser; I am worthless; I will never be loved."

The positive side of a negative blueprint

Oftentimes, a negative blueprint becomes the driving force in a person's life that propels him to great heights of achievement. For example, someone close to me is driven by the constant need for recognition, whether in public or private life. He is your typical over achiever, who had a phenomenal rise in corporate America, and who rubs shoulders with the leaders of the free world.

Notwithstanding the outer appearance of self assuredness and security, this man is forever striving for approval from his wife, his colleagues, and everyone he meets. He measures his own success by what others are saying about him. He will go to the other end of the world – literally, to receive recognition from someone – a handshake from an emperor, an audience with a king, a blessing from the Pope, a signed photograph with someone important, or even just another plaque to be mounted on his wall.

This leader of a billion dollar enterprise will ask his wife to approve his clothing "How do I look, my dear?" every time they go out in public. When entering a room, banquet or otherwise, he will be the last to go in after everyone is already seated to be sure that he is "recognized".

I often wondered what drives this man to have his need of recognition fulfilled over and over again. When I asked him once about his childhood, he told me that his father was never there for him as a young child and that he was always on his own.

His blueprint became quite clear to me then. Essentially, he is saying to his (long departed) father and to the rest of the world: "Notice me, see what I can do, tell me how brilliant I am, how deserving I am of your recognition and your love, because if you don't tell me, I feel worthless".

The correlation between early childhood trauma and serious illness

Many studies have been done on the correlation between early childhood trauma and serious illnesses in later life. These studies on more than 30,000 people prove that there is a very real cause and effect syndrome. A child that has been told a thousand times by its parents "You are a pain in the neck!" hears these words, believes them and repeats them subconsciously over and over again, and sure enough, the body responds to this command and creates a very real pain in the neck, in the form of a tumor, a hemorrhage, a disease of the spinal column, even cancer.

Children who have lived in an atmosphere of hostility and physical abuse, often develop heart disease, cancer and chronic lung disorders in later life. Many become heavy smokers, drug abusers and alcoholics – often to simply numb the pain of their terrible childhood. Trusting another human being is difficult, if not impossible for them and as a result, they have short lived relationships and marriages that end in divorce.

Dr. Harold Bloomfeld states that "these risk factors increase chronic adrenaline secretion. Over time, this can tear at heart muscle fiber, produce cardiac arrythmias and result in sudden death. Hypercortisol secretion is the second stage of response to these risk factors. The cortisol is good in an acute emergency, but over time it lowers your immune response so it leaves you much more vulnerable not only to colds and infections but cancer as well. Individuals with adverse childhood experiences are much more likely to have a chronic stress physiology and may not even know it because they have always felt that way."

The body-mind-spirit connection

The body-mind-spirit connection becomes more evident as we delve deeper into this subject.

> ➤ Karen, a teenager, is consumed by guilt feelings because of something that has happened a decade earlier. When

her parents divorced, Karen, as many children do, took the blame on her little shoulders and decided that she was bad and that she was the reason for her parents' breakup. She is living with this self imposed guilt and it is affecting her ability to relate to her classmates, to form friendships and to excel academically.

➤ Maddie on the other hand, is experiencing a different emotion. She feels shame. She was sexually molested as a child and has kept this secret to herself all her life. She feels that she **is** wrong (as opposed to having done something wrong which she should feel guilty about), while everyone else is normal. Her belief that something is wrong with her expands with time to "I am not pretty enough, I am not smart enough, I am not good enough, I am worthless".

Maddie's spirit is broken and healing cannot begin until she discovers her blueprint and learns that she internalized the trauma of her childhood - done to her by someone else – and made it her own. When she lets go of this falsehood she will be ready to draft a new blueprint for herself and live a life without shame.

The perils of disgrace

Simpler, though no less devastating negative blueprints are formed every day through careless comments, unkind acts or ridicule by parents, family members or other children. Very often the cause of disgrace is loss of bladder or bowel control brought on by fright or accident that evolves into much more than embarrassment:

Little Julia has to pee. She is certain of it. For the past hour she's been holding it in and the pressure is getting worse by the minute. She presses her thighs together, then crosses her legs, she even cubs her hands over her private parts when she's sure her mother won't notice. She's in the back seat of the family car, "Mommy, I've got to go to the bathroom" she cries for the 10th time.

"I told you you've got to wait until we get there! There is no bathroom here – so stop whining about it!" comes the shouting reply from her mother in the driver's seat. "But I can't! I can't, I really have to go!" cries little Julia – and then it happens. The car brakes suddenly and Julia feels the warm liquid oozing from her body and wetting her beautiful dress. She shrieks with fear – fear of her mother's anger, fear of being punished, fear of once again having disappointed and disobeyed her mother, and deep down fear of losing her mother's love.

Her blueprint is formed: I'm a failure; I'll always disappoint my mother; my mother will never love me, the world is horrible without love … Imagine Julia's feelings as she grows up truly believing that the world is a horrible place – just because she peed into her panties one sad day when she was five years old… She does not know why she feels that way, and this, of course, is the cruelty of the blueprint.

Johnny is going to school today and this is the first time he's on the school bus. He does not know what he's in for. There are kids much older than he and they look mean. One of them particularly – he's sitting behind Johnny and he's pulling his hair. Johnny cries out in pain, he does not know what to do, so he slouches in his seat and tries to make himself smaller. The big bully behind him just laughs and is now pounding with his fists on Johnny's head. Two other kids join in the fun. They pick on his shirt, one grabs his school bag and they heckle and poke him. Johnny is so scared that he pees in his pants.

The bus stops and the kids get out. Johnny is the last one to leave because he is embarrassed about the wet spot on his pants. As he steps down from the bus, the bully and his buddies are waiting for him. And that's when something happens to his psyche – the fear and embarrassment turn into anger, hate and rage in a split second. Johnny's hands form fists, he lunges at the bully and pounces on him so fast the other two don't know what's happening. Johnny hammers blows to the bully's face and nose and soon there is blood everywhere....

Johnny walks away from this episode with a blueprint that has him believe that aggressive behavior is the only way to survive in a hostile world. He grows up becoming a bully himself and uses violence to get his way.

The pain of ridicule is no laughing matter

Whether you were ridiculed as a young child, in your adolescent years, or even during your adult life, you know that it is a very serious matter. Regardless of whether it took the form of bullying or meanness passed off as "jokes," you learned that being ridiculed is not something to laugh about at all, in fact – it's painful. This type of torment is something no one should have to endure and it leaves a lasting impression on those who have gone through it.

If you were ridiculed as a child, you probably feel "less" about yourself than you actually are. It is only human nature for a person to absorb the cruel things which are said about him or her – and, in many cases, is left with the feeling that perhaps those remarks or taunts were true. In other words, you internalized the pain of ridicule; and you may have begun to use what was said about you as the "measure" of who you really are.

When you define yourself based on someone else's cruel remarks it cuts away at your self-esteem. When you define yourself based on someone else's cruel remarks it cuts away at your self-esteem. When someone has ridiculed your appearance, your abilities, or your talents, it can cause you to lower your opinion of yourself. And to make things worse, you may tend to define yourself as you were told you were, and now do not have a very clear view of the person you actually are. Ridicule damages your self-esteem, as well as your sense of personal identity!

Parents are by far the greatest originators of negative blueprints for their children

I was at a seminar recently when a lady shared how she discovered her blueprint. She had been at her mother's house and had noted a broken fixture in the kitchen. As she set out to fix it, her mother came by and said "Oh dear, you don't have to do this if it's too hard." "No, Mom, I'm ok, I'm fixing it" she replied and continued. But somehow the tools she had at hand were not the right ones and things progressed poorly. Mother came back with another "Dear, you don't have to do this if it's too hard".

By the third "You don't have to do this if it's too hard" it finally hit her: she had been living by her mother's instructions – don't do something if it's too hard.

Her mother, in her own desire to make life easier for her daughter had brainwashed her to shy away from anything that was difficult. She now understood why her life had taken the turns it did, why she had not achieved her goals and dreams...

Anna's Story

My friend Anna recently moved to Florida and purchased a lovely home of typical open design with lots of windows, high ceilings and plenty of sunshine. I had seen pictures of the model house and was looking forward to my first visit.

Yet when I walked into the living room the first time I could not believe my eyes. Heavy drapes obscured the wall to wall windows, allowing just a narrow slit for sunshine to come in. The walls had been painted green and beige – pleasant enough colors and well co-ordinated, but much too dark.

The guest bedroom where I was staying was a very dark maroon color. I felt suffocated. When I turned on the light, energy saver bulbs greeted me with barely enough strength to equal a 25 watt incandescent bulb. My entire visit disturbed me enough to want to solve the mystery – why was my friend afraid of the light? We know each other well enough, so I simply asked her, and Anna told me her story:

When Anna was just a little girl, her parents had a disagreement which prompted her mother to pack up her two children and take them to live with her parents in the country. Anna was devastated. She did not want to leave the family home. She had practiced for a piano recital at school and she wanted to play. She begged to stay, but her mother said no. At least, if she had to come along, could she take her piano with her? Of course not, that was out of the question, her mother said.

The family lived in Indonesia and travel was difficult at that time. They had to take the bus to the railway station and then wait a long time for the train to arrive. Everyone was tired and hungry and Anna was scared. She did not know what happened to her Daddy. She was scared that she would never see him again. Deep inside her heart she knew that it was all her fault that he was not with them. She did not know what she had done in particular, but she knew she was bad and that she should not have asked about the piano...

The train arrived and the family got on. Just as they were seated in their cabin, the sun started to set and with every klunkedy-klunk of the train, it was getting darker and darker outside. With every disappearing ray of the sun, deeper shadows formed inside the cabin and inside Anna's soul. Darkness was closing in on her and with it the feeling that the world was collapsing, that she would never see the sun again. She was being punished - punished to a life without sunshine, without laughter, without happiness.

And so it was. The moment Anna believed that the sun had set to punish her, her blueprint was formed, and for as long as she held on to this belief, she lived in darkness both physically and emotionally. Dark colors characterized her physical environment and depression became a recurring problem in her life.

And here is a story that will make you cringe at the thoughtlessness of adults when it comes to upholding traditions:

Krampus Day

St. Nicholas is a children's saint who is honored in Austria on December 6th. According to legend, God rewarded Nicholas' generosity by sending him to earth each year to bring gifts to all good children. We call St. Nicholas "Niklaus" or "Nicolo".

He looks like a bishop, with his flowing robes, his tall pointed bishop's hat and the crozier, the symbol of authority. He has little resemblance to the Santa Claus of the Western world, who is depicted as a jolly good fellow with a big pot belly and an infectious Ho-Ho-Ho laugh.

But Nicolo does not come alone – he is accompanied by Krampus, a strange and frightening creature that looks like the devil. He dresses in fur and wears a scary mask with a long red tongue. Krampus carries chains and whips made out of twigs to beat the bad children, and he has a big bucket on his back to carry away the really bad boys and girls, so that Nicolo does not get confused as to who deserves his gifts of goodies.

It is said that St. Nicholas never allows Krampus to harm anyone. But little boys and girls do not know this, and the terror they feel when they believe that they will be taken away by this horrible creature can be devastating and very harmful indeed. Here is what happened to me when I encountered Krampus for the first time:

It is late, past bedtime, and I am scared. All day long my mother has reminded me that it is Krampus day. I don't know what that means, but my instincts tell me that it cannot be good. So I cower under the dining room table, hidden behind the long table cloth, and pray that nobody will find me.

The doorbell rings and I recognize my mother's friend Herr Biel. I don't like him; he always smells like cigarettes and has yellow fingers and teeth from all that smoking. I hear him call my name, but I don't answer. Heavy steps circle the room and they zero in on my hiding place. The table cloth is lifted and the yellow clawed hands grab me by the arms and pull me out.

"So, there you are! Why are you hiding? Have you been a bad girl? Must be so... You know what happens to bad little girls, don't you? Ha?"

I protest: " I've been good, I've been good, I promise!"

"Krampus comes tonight and he punishes bad little girls with his whips and then takes them away in his big bucket! He will be here any minute now", says Herr Biel and shakes me for good measure.

"What do you have to say for yourself, young lady? Your mother tells me that you have been a bad girl, that you don't pay her any mind, that you don't eat your cabbage, that you fight with your sister, that you...., that you..." I don't hear the accusations any more. I am nauseated and pull away with all my might, but to no avail – the claws are holding me tightly.

"I've been good! I am a good girl!" I cry "Please don't let him take me away, please, please, I'll be good, I promise, I prom-ise!!!"

And then deafening sounds come from the stairway heading up to our apartment. The rattling of chains chills my bones. Herr Biel drags me to the front door – I am scream-ing and kicking, trying desper-ately to escape. "Mutti, Mutti, help me! I am scared! I don't want to...."

The words get stuck in my throat as I glimpse the huge

and grotesque figure standing in the doorway. I see shaggy black fur, I see chains, I see silver whips, I see the bucket and I see a pair of red horns on the devil's head. By now I am clinging for dear life to the legs of Herr Biel. I am sobbing hysterically for fear, screaming at the top of my lungs "don't take me away, don't take me away, I'll be good, I'll be good, I promise, I promise!"

Krampus lifts his massive arms and menacingly rattles the chains. He thrashes the air in my direction with the silver whips – and that's when I lose it and pee in my panties...

I don't remember how I was rescued from this predicament; all I remember are the terror I felt that night and the absolute belief I carried with me from this encounter with Krampus – that I was a wicked girl. Wicked girls have to be punished, and I learned to practice self punishment and self doubt all my life.

I cannot imagine why parents would want to traumatize their children with such nonsense. Unfortunately many do. It is a great blessing when responsible parents know how to create a safe environment for their children and to shower them with affection and love, which lead to positive blueprints.

Positive blueprints

Positive blueprints are formed differently. There is no trauma attached to them and therefore exists not one single event that is imprinted in a child's mind. Instead, positive blueprints are formed through constant positive suggestions, praises, and most of all, expressions of love. A hug, a pat on the head, a caress of the cheek, even a simple smile conveys the message of approval to the child.

Here is an example of a positive blueprint:

This little girl and her mother are reading a picture book together. The little girl sits on her Mom's lap and her small fingers trace the pictures as her Mom reads out loud and moves from page to page. "Mommy", she says, "what's this?" she points to a picture on the page. "This", says her Mom, "is an airplane. It's way up there in the sky and it flies from place to place just as the birds do." "Can I fly in an airplane?"

"Yes, of course you can, sweetheart" answers her Mom. "No, Mommy, I mean, can I fly the airplane myself?" insists the little girl.

"Yes, my love, you can – you can do anything you want to do when you grow up. You are so smart and brave and you'll be a real star someday. You could even be an astronaut." "What's an astronaut?" "Well, that's a pilot who flies to the stars" "Oh, goody, goody, I want to fly to the stars, Mommy!" "Well, then you will, my child, then you will..."

This little girl will grow up knowing that she is smart, that she has the support of her family and that she will succeed in whatever she attempts. She will have a high self esteem and live her life to her fullest potential. Her mind is not bruised; it is nurtured with love and support.

...positive blueprints are formed through constant positive suggestions, praises, and most of all, expressions of love.

This love will also grow and will support every aspect of her mind and life; it will not pause until it is strong and powerful to stave off negative thoughts and emotions so they never have a chance to influence her in any way.

Everyone is in search of love. When love is withheld from a child by its parents, whether through neglect, by circumstances or willfully, the child creates a loving environment in his or her imagination, like I did when I was still in grade school – you may recall that the words "I love you" were never voiced in our house...

I remember back to my childhood – I must have been in the third of fourth grade. I followed my teacher from school. I found her apartment building, I climbed up the steps in the dingily lit staircase and I stood in front of her apartment door, heart pounding, not knowing what to do. I did not dare ring the bell – what would I say to her? Why was I here?

As I was standing there, I imagined what was on the other side of the door. In my mind's eye I could see the bright sunshine lit entry way, leading to her living room – there were plants everywhere, and the sofa was soft and inviting and there she was, relaxing, watching TV with her feet up on the chair and the kitty cat curled up in her lap. I imagined being that kitty cat, with my teacher's hands caressing me, holding me and telling me that she loved me, that I was precious to her and that I made her life full of joy and happiness.

I cannot begin to tell you how happy I am that my son Paul has turned out to be an incredibly thoughtful and gifted father. He instinctively knows how to interact with his children in a most loving and tender way which both assures them of his unconditional love while confirming his authority and responsibility as their parent. And he does this in spite of the fact that I, his mother, was the very cause of his negative blueprint that left him feeling abandoned and in search for love.

But more about this in the next chapter...

To prepare yourself for the journey you are going to take in a little while to discover your own blueprint, start by studying the behaviors of the people around you. Have you ever asked yourself why your friend Bob gets so agitated every time someone mentions his sister? Or why your aunt Lilly never goes into the water swimming? Or why your cousin Henrietta complains to you about her love life every time she sees you? How about your realtor Tony who talks incessantly to the point that you can't get a word in – what makes these people behave the way they do?

Exercise

Everyone has a story and for most people the origin of that story was some event in their childhood. For this exercise, imagine what this event might have been for your friend Bob, your aunt Lilly and cousin Henrietta and all the people around you that you want to think about. Of course, substitute my examples for people you know personally.

Using your imagination to "see" the possible events that could have triggered the blueprint of others will enrich you in many ways and prepare you for your own discovery.

Chapter 1 - How Blueprints Are Formed

∽

A teacher affects eternity:

he can never tell where his influence stops.

Henry Adams

∽

Chapter 2

How Your Blueprint Defines Your Life and Influences the Lives of Those Around You

Influence refers to the ability to indirectly affect the actions of others. We influence others by our entire personality. Every word, every gesture, every smile or frown conveys our feelings about ourselves and every event that touches us. We radiate vibrations (energy) that reach others and influences their emotions and in turn their words and actions.

Think back to a time when you accidentally walked into a room where an argument was in progress, between your parents perhaps, your siblings, children, co-workers, friends or strangers. Even if no one was speaking, you instantly knew something negative was going on because the air felt as though it could be cut with a knife. This vibration (energy) influenced you immediately in one way or another.

Perhaps you walked away not wanting to feel the negative vibes, or you felt ashamed or wanted to help the folks sort out their problem. Either way, you were affected by the argument, which in turn influenced your day, your week, your view of the people involved, your view of your own relationship with them, perhaps your feeling about the subject of the argument, how you felt about the place where it was going on, etc. Everything changed, if only in a subtle way. You were not the same person after the argument than you were before.

Hundreds of books have been written on how to influence others. Influence is an art to be learned when you are in the business of selling a product or service – your measure of success will be the number of sales you generate by convincing others to buy what you have to offer. Knowing how to consciously influence others is indeed a very useful skill. Unknowingly influencing others in a negative way, however, is not such a good thing.

Few books, if any, focus on negative influences practiced by people who live by their negative blueprint. It is very hard to positively influence someone in views different from your own when you see the entire world through blueprint shaded glasses. A father, who believes that rich people cannot be trusted, will not teach his children to seek the company of rich people nor will he teach them how to become rich. A mother, who was molested as a child, will not have a healthy attitude towards sex to pass on to her daughter. Of course, both father and mother in these examples could have many positive influences on their children – just not in the areas shaded by their blueprint.

Everything you think, speak or act is based on the belief structure anchored in your subconscious...

Everything you think, speak or act is based on the belief structure anchored in your subconscious mind where it was engraved during your childhood. You cannot escape your destiny until you change your blueprint. Like I could not escape my destiny – I had to become Superwoman, the professional who could do everything and anything better than her male colleagues; the mother who could raise her children and have a career at the same time; the woman who valued achievement above feelings and emotions…

A day in the life of Superwoman:

I am sitting in the partner's office at Price Waterhouse and we are making the final changes to a very important proposal to the government of Puerto Rico for the re-design of operating procedures for the Social Services Department. The presentation is scheduled for 2 p.m. It is now 11:30 am. The receptionist sticks her head in the door and points to me: "You have a phone call on Line 1". I cringe. I hate it when they transfer my calls into the partner's office. I pick up the phone: It's the kindergarten nurse. "Your son has just thrown up all over the floor in class; he's sick and has to be picked up from school now!"

As I contemplate what to do, whether to tell the partner the truth or come up with another excuse for why I have to leave at this crucial moment, the receptionist is once more in my face – with a sterner look this time: "You have another call on Line 1". I glance at the partner and the other managers in the room and pick up the phone a second time. This time it's my neighbor – "one of your dogs got out and he's charging up and down the beach. You better come and get him before someone gets hurt!"

We have two Dobermans and the male dog, RobRoy, is trained as an attack dog – so I fear for the worst. While he's normally a gentle dog, out alone he could be provoked by any stranger and then all hell would break lose. "Where is my husband? Why can't he take care of the dog?" "Well, he's out on the boat and can't be reached." Terrific! Another disaster that I have to take care of myself...

I mumble some lame excuse to the group, swear I'll be back in time for the proposal presentation and rush out the door. I run to my car – thank God I remembered to get gas last night – and make a quick decision which way to turn first – to the child or the dog. If I get to my son first, then I can't leave him alone in the house while chasing the dog. So the dog comes first. I charge down the streets, cutting off cars left and right and ignore their angry honking and make it home.

I park the car on top of the curb and race out to the beach – no dog in sight. My heart sinks – what do I do now?

I get back into my car and slowly drive along the beach until the street comes to an end. I turn around and try the other side – there, a black dot in the distance, no, two black dots... as I come closer, they turn out to be RobRoy and a big mutt in a dog fight. I yell and whistle and call RobRoy – to no avail. He is charging at the mutt, fangs snarling, hair raised on his back – you get the picture. There is nothing to do but to separate the dogs before they kill each other.

I take off my shoes (high heels, of course) and run out onto the beach in my stocking feet. I slap RobRoy on his rump and grab the mutt by his tail. Both are now snarling at me. I back off – but too late. The mutt is now charging at me and the force of his attack throws me to the ground. We roll in the sand, I grab a hold of his collar and now I'm the boss. I jerk him into submission and catch RobRoy by his collar before he takes off again. Oh-no, there is sand all over my clothes and – what's that? – there is blood too. Now I note the big gash in my forearm, must have happened while wrestling the dog in the sand. I let the mutt go and run with RobRoy to the car. He jumps in, front seat of course, shakes his butt, and now there is sand all over the car as well. Oh well, can't worry about that now – we have to get Paul.

I arrive at the school by 12:30 p.m. – good, still enough time to make the 2:00 p.m. presentation I think. Something is nagging at me – what did I forget? Oh, my God, the baby-sitter! I dash to the nurse's office "where's Paul?" She gives me the look-over that says it all and then leads me to the cot where my poor little darling is sleeping. He looks ashen and exhausted from his ordeal. I leave him there for the moment and charge to the nurse's telephone (we did not have cell phones in Puerto Rico in 1973). I call Anna, no answer. I call Juanita, no answer. And then Isabel and leave a message.

Now I am getting really nervous – the time is ticking away, it is now 1 p.m. Paul wakes up, sees me and starts crying. I pick him up and console him. My fifth call reaches Renata and my pleas for help get through to her – she agrees to watch him for a few hours. I promise her double pay if she makes it to our house in ten minutes. Paul in my arms, I get back to the car and find that RobRoy has chewed through the front seat leather in defiance of having been left alone in the car. A big sigh escapes my lips. I feel defeated. Nothing is going right today – no matter what I do, I can't win!

I plump Paul on the seat and race home. Renata is waiting for me. I hand over Paul, give him a kiss "Mommy will be home soon" and haste to the bedroom. I throw another outfit into a bag and remember to call the office: "I'll meet you at the presentation site", I tell them and run back to my car. Five minutes to 2 p.m. I arrive there and miraculously find a parking space just outside the front door. I run up the stairs to the second floor – elevator takes too long – and head for the Ladies' Room. A mini-sponge bath later I emerge in my new outfit and assume my role of Senior Manager as I enter the conference room to give my presentation.

It's a big success and we get the engagement.

Sounds familiar? Haven't we seen this scene somewhere before? Ah yes – it was George Clooney and Michelle Pfeifer in "One Fine Day"! Different story – same scenario. Yep! That was me alright – one day in the life of Superwoman: professional, mother, wife, housekeeper, dog trainer, juggler of emotions, Jack of all trades, and master of none.

I felt totally inadequate, like I was skimming the surface...

I felt totally inadequate, like I was skimming the surface, treading water or walking on thin ice, wondering when everything was going to collapse under my feet. I was expected to be all that and I managed to play this Superwoman role most of the time, but inside I didn't feel it. I worried all the time that someone would find out that I was a fraud, a wanna-be, someone who lacked the credentials to be a true professional. Why did I feel this way? Well, it's true, I didn't go to college for 4 years, I skipped the Bachelor's and went straight into the Masters Degree program.

I studied at night school because I had a full time job during the day. I had a live-in housekeeper who practically raised my children the first five years of their lives. And I felt guilty about that, gut wrenchingly guilty. But I did not know what else to do – the job was demanding and I had to do it better than everyone (all men, naturally) else, because only then would I be accepted and considered "one of them"…

Of course, what I saw and felt then was shaded by the tinted lenses of my blueprint. All others saw – and what I see now that the glasses have come off – is a wonderful success story, not a near disaster. I can laugh now at the absurdity of it all, me chasing a couple of mad dogs and ending up making a presentation to the Ministry with sand in my underpants.

I was in fact Superwoman that day, I did not just pretend to be. I am proud now of both my dog mastery and my acting skills that allowed me to carry off a most convincing professional performance when it counted the most. Amazing what a change in mindset can do! Then I saw myself as a loser who was lucky to have gotten away with a charade – now I see myself as a leader, someone who in her early years already knew how to overcome obstacles that life threw in her way and to come out a winner every time!

Looking back at that time, I realize that all my actions were driven by this need to be strong, to be powerful and invincible like a man – because men can do anything they want…I was living according to my blueprint: life is not safe for a woman. I did everything I could to move into a man's world and considered my roles as wife and mother as necessary evils to be overcome in order to get ahead – they were mere side shows to the main event.

I was going to be a partner at Price Waterhouse and the fact that I was a woman was irrelevant, even though, had I been successful in achieving this goal, I would have been the first woman partner in that firm. Alas, it was not to be, but that's another story.

The funny thing is that I did not really want to be a partner at an accounting firm – I just wanted to belong to the "club", the boy's club, the club where you get the key to the executive bathroom, where you know "you have arrived". Inside I knew that I would never be truly happy and fulfilled in this job.

Happiness was elusive, in fact I did not know what it was. Being happy meant having all the latest toys, getting through the day, not having fights at home, fooling the neighbors, the boss, the co-workers and friends, that I was on top of the world and being able to brag about my accomplishments to family back in Austria – but real, unadulterated happiness was elusive, an unknown feeling – hence nothing could ever measure up to it.

Only one thing was satisfied – the blueprint. For as long as I lived and acted out my blueprint, I felt – artificially - fulfilled.

Our influence over others

So what does all of this mean? Well, like it or not, everything we do influences someone. Under the power of my blueprint during my Superwoman years, I influenced a lot of people, not all positively I have to admit.

> ➤ First of all, my children: they grew up with a non sup-
> portive mother, who had other priorities than to care for
> them the way a loving, warm fuzzy Mom should. They
> saw lots of money and toys and were influenced to be-
> lieve that money could buy their happiness – an easy as-
> sumption to make as a child when there is instant gratifi-
> cation in return for a temper tantrum.
>
> On the other hand, I did influence them to believe that
> they could do whatever they wanted if they set their mind
> to it. Unfortunately in our family, there was a tug of war

between my blueprint values and those of their father, who lived by the motto "Handwerk hat goldenen Boden" (German, meaning "manual labor makes golden floors") and who, being the stronger man, had a greater influence on them when it came to choice of education, study and academic accomplishments.

➤ My ex-husband: now here is a scary thought; I have influenced him in many ways from the day we met. He followed me from Austria to Canada to Puerto Rico, giving up his own comfort zone as blue collar worker to be ultimately drawn into the life of a motivated career woman who was embarrassed by his lack of culture, and disenchanted by his unwillingness to grow at her pace. We were batting heads all the time.

There was enormous tension brought on by differences of opinion on how to raise the children

There was enormous tension brought on by differences of opinion on how to raise the children – he believed in the old school of discipline, whereas I had a much softer touch. Only he can tell whether my influence over him was positive or negative. Of course, from my point of view I tried to make him a better person – but one who was more likely to be accepted in my world, not his.

We were mismatched from the beginning, having married for all the wrong reasons. I married him to get away from home – he was my ticket out of a place that made me very uncomfortable. The daily reminder in the form of my mother that being a woman was not safe, coupled with my inner conflict that as a woman I too was vulnerable and could be hurt at any moment, was too much and I had to get out. Why Wil married me I don't know, but love was not a factor.

➤ Co-workers: At Price Waterhouse, co-workers generally regarded me either as a threat or as a nuisance, depending on their own level of confidence. Those who saw me as a threat worried that I would get promoted ahead of them. They saw it a challenge to beat me in billable hours – the performance measure at PW – and to work longer hours than I did. At the time I felt challenged too, but also insecure and left out. Why would they feel the need to compete with me? I hated competition and would have much preferred to work together as team mates, solve client's problems and have fun in the process.

But since they wanted challenges, I could outperform all of them and win. After all, I was living according to my blueprint, and it would not allow me to deviate. My reluctant influence over my co-workers made them work harder than they would have otherwise. I exercised leadership without ever knowing it. Simply by being me, I coerced my co-workers into doing better work, and together we served our clients better. PW got more clients and made more money – everyone was better off – except those co-workers, of course, who thought I was a nuisance. They did not last long.

➤ Friends: Friends were hard to read. I was never sure whether they liked me or tolerated me or used me. Of course, all my friends were male, except for a few friends Wil and I shared as a couple. I had few women friends during my Superwoman years. I had nothing in common with women, except for the ones who were mothers like me.

When my children were very young, I was caught up in the motherhood role for a while, but this faded fast once they started going to school and I had a live-in housekeeper/nanny. Since I spent little time with women I cannot say that I have influenced them in any way.

Men, on the other hand, I know I have influenced. Some admired me and some were intimidated by me. Often I asked myself in the past – what do they want from me? Is this a sexual attraction? Why are they hanging around me? Ultimately though I think they sought out my friendship because they saw value in it, and that felt good.

I chose to write about being a Superwoman because I believe you and I have a lot in common. I may have had more color in my life than some of you because of my background, heritage and a bit of luck, but ultimately we Superwomen struggle daily with the numerous obligations imposed on us that cause conflicts: how can we be nurturing and supporting and loving and at the same time tough and demanding and nerveless when it comes to business negotiations? Lucky are the women these days who can afford to have only the job of being a good home maker...

Exercise

I want you to think about your own life now. Think about your job, your family, your friends and your relationships with everyone you meet. Make a list of all the people you interact with on a daily basis, whether these are significant interactions – like with your spouse or boss at work – and then think about how you influence them. You will be surprised at the results of this exercise:

Name _____ Relationship _____

How you influence him/her _____

_____

_____

Name _____ Relationship _____

How you influence him/her _____

_____

_____

Name _____ Relationship _____

How you influence him/her _____

_____

_____

Did you include on your list the office boy who delivers your mail, the school bus driver who catches a glimpse of you in your house coat as you wave your children good-bye, or the toll booth cashier, who surely could use a smile from you as you zip by? When you really think about your interactions with others you will realize that you influence everyone you come in contact with every day of your life.

Add to this all the people whom you know, but only see once in a while – they may be thinking about you frequently if they are family or good friends; or they may think of you only sometime when a flash of memory crosses their mind. The simple fact that you have met at one time has influenced them – and you – in some way.

For example, the office boy might admire you and yearn to become an important person like you; he might be inspired by your every action and dream about sitting in your chair one day. Or, he might say to himself – no way that I'll be a slave to 9-5 office hours all my life! I'd better start thinking about something else to do!

The school bus driver might dream about his own wife and family after he observes you seeing your children off to school. He might feel happy to be blessed with a loving wife or sad because he has only memories left of her. No matter how he feels – the point is that by your sheer presence in his life at this very moment, you influence his feelings and perhaps the direction his life will take because of them.

When you have completed your list and analysis, ask yourself another question: are you a positive influence on the people who are close and important to you? If not, what would it take to change that? We'll talk about this some more in a later chapter.

My blueprint forced me to live a life of inner struggle... My blueprint forced me to live a life of inner struggle: drawn on the one side to become strong and powerful because only then would I feel safe; and then there was the pull on the other side that said "I can't make a difference, I'm useless, I'm powerless". For every success in my life I found an excuse to feel inadequate. Life was good – life was bad.

I was on an emotional treadmill, push myself up and tear myself down again – up and down, up and down, a never ending cycle. This yo-yo syndrome also manifested itself in my weight – feel good, down came the weight, feel bad – up it went, up and down in tandem with my emotions. I ultimately conquered this struggle, but only after changing my blueprint.

I promised to tell you about my son Paul, whom I influenced negatively more than I thought possible – and all because of my blueprint. It was only yesterday that Paul shared his secret with me. And when he did I was overcome with a feeling of deep sadness, and once again, gut wrenching guilt.

Paul's Story

Paul and I have always been very close in spite of having lived apart for most of our lives. I am eternally grateful for this closeness and love, because all could have ended up differently…

Paul was just 8 years old when my marriage with his father finally came to an end. I had known five years before that we were hopelessly mismatched and that there was no long term future for us, but guilt feelings kept me from moving on. There was the guilt of breaking up the marriage, leaving Wil, who was not working at the time, without the means to continue living a life of luxury to which he had become accustomed with me. This was coupled with the guilt of having uprooted him from Austria only to abandon him 16 years later in Puerto Rico – irrational guilt, of course, because life goes on and change is inevitable – but guilt it was nevertheless.

And then there were the children, my daughter Fritzi and my son Paul, who were 13 and 8 at the time if the divorce. Their lives hung in the balance and I chose to follow my blueprint instead of my heart and duty to them as their mother – I did not fight for them in the divorce. I chose the easy way out – paying their father alimony to take care of them while I was free to pursue my career. Fritzi was already living with her Godparents in Canada, so only Paul was affected, and I thought he could handle it. In my defense I must say that Wil would not have agreed to the divorce if he did not get custody of Paul, and continuing our marriage was not acceptable to me at that point.

During the succeeding few years, Paul and I met once or twice per year for a couple of weeks, as I had transferred from Puerto Rico to Washington, D.C. to work at the World Bank. Wil remarried only six months after our divorce, so very soon Paul had a step mother barely 10 years older than himself. I knew that these were unhappy times for him, so I arranged to send him to boarding school in Switzerland once he was old enough (at 14) to tell his father that he wanted to leave him. And life took its course for Paul from then on, with college, marriage and children of his own.

When I discovered my blueprint, I shared my experience with Paul and told him that I was writing this book. He read these chapters as they were evolving, and that started his own journey of discovery. He had issues in his own marriage and needed to know whether these issues were attributable to him, his wife or their relationship.

And then one day – he knew. He called me to share his discovery: "Mom, I know my blueprint! I never thought it could be that simple – everything fits together! All my emotions, my confusion and searching, all are explained now."

"Mom, my blueprint was formed – when you left!"

And instantly I knew that he was right. My leaving him at the age of 8 shaded his view of the world. He felt the deep loss of abandonment (it is incredible that his love for me survived this feeling!); betrayal, as the life he knew was shattered with the arrival of a new, young step mother; loneliness, because all the people he loved were far away (his mother and sister); and hopelessness, as he struggled to understand how his life could have been turned upside down so fast and so cruelly. Added to this blueprint were blueprints formed at the hands of his father, who excelled in over-disciplining his son and never learned how to praise and support him.

In his adult life, Paul's blueprint had him searching for ful-fillment in all the areas he had been robbed of it in his child-hood – love, trust, companionship, hope and recognition for a job well done.

Fritzi's Story

I would be greatly amiss here if I did not also tell you my daughter's story. Fritzi got the short end of the stick from the moment she was born. She entered the world the wrong way (she was a breech birth and came feet first) and, beautiful as she was with her big dark eyes, her world was upside down ever since.

I clearly remember the moment when the doctors at the hospital told me that I had a baby girl: I shook my head over and over again and groaned "no, no, no". My reaction was totally unexpected – even for me. I did not know what had come over me. I felt I was being punished, but for what I did not know.

Now of course, it is quite clear to me. Giving birth to a female child was unthinkably cruel! The horrors that I witnessed when my mother was beaten up surfaced at that moment, raising big warning signs and a foreboding that the same fate would befall my child, all because I had had no courage and was incapable of help-ing my mother when she needed me the most. This twisted lie that had become my blueprint was now reaching out to engulf the life of yet another innocent child, my own sweet daughter.

Fritzi was a beautiful little girl who deserved to be loved and cher-ished. Yet, sadly, she was not. Her father, ever the disciplinarian, never knew how to be a loving father; and I, her mother, found it difficult to be close to her. Her mere presence made me feel inse-cure. Every time Wil punished her for something I felt horrible but could do nothing to stop him, nor could I console and love her. My blueprint was confirmed – women were vulnerable and the world was not a safe place for women. Why was I burdened with a female child to protect when I had more than enough trouble to keep myself safe in this cruel world?

When Fritzi was five years old, her brother Paul was born, and things got worse for her, much worse. Not only was there the normal sibling rivalry and insecurity when a newborn captures the parent's attention away from the only child, there was searing jealousy in Fritzi. She knew instantly that Paul was loved and she was not. With every day her resentment against him grew stronger and her behavior at home and at school grew worse. Over the next few years, Fritzi changed from the sweet little girl to a loudmouthed, difficult and bossy girl who was constantly in trouble.

When Fritzi was 12 years old, she declared that she hated Puerto Rico where we were living at the time, and that she wanted to go back to Canada, where she was born. I gladly accepted her proposition and sent her to live with her Godparents in Toronto. It was the easy way out for me, and true to my blueprint, I took it.

From then on, our relationship deteriorated more and more, which should be of no surprise to anyone reading these lines. It was as if we had gone through a divorce, where nothing was left to be said after the judge drops the gravel and the parties go their own way. For two decades we did not speak with each other.

And then the miracle happened. First there was a short, unimportant contact, then a phone call here and there, a brief letter perhaps and a greeting card at Christmas. Fritzi was an adult by then, in her early thirties and living in a steady relationship with her partner. I had remarried, left the World Bank and was running my own company. We both had matured and when the opportunity arose for a talk about the past, we took it and slowly started to mend our relationship.

I, the guilty party, asked for forgiveness, and Fritzi, the injured one, had the grace and decency to extend it, for which I will be forever grateful. At that time, I still did not know what had prompted my aversion against her, I just knew that I had wronged her terribly and that she did not deserve the cold treatment she had gotten from me. Since then, we have been building our relationship and now have a loving and caring bond that gets stronger every day.

As I had done with Paul, I told Fritzi that I was writing this book and asked if she wanted to be featured in it. She did not hesitate, and as the memories came back to her, so did the tears and revelations about her past that I knew nothing about.

Here are Fritzi's words:

Mom, I remember clearly my resentment against Paul. He was getting all the attention from you – he was your pride and joy. I took out my anger on him and when we got into fights, I got punished the most simply because I was the older one.

At school and everywhere I went, I was looking for attention. That's how I got into trouble all the time. I was equating any kind of attention with love. I was sexually abused in my school; I started taking drugs at a very early age; I once took Dad's cigarettes, went up on the roof and smoked the entire pack (and of course got caught). In Puerto Rico you had to come to school and meet with the school psychiatrist because they found my stash of dirty magazines. And then there were the older men who exposed themselves to me on the beach where we lived. I got obscene phone calls at home from men who knew that we kids were alone in the house.

Not getting attention all these years is what made me so loud and boisterous with people to make sure that I was being noticed. I talked to anyone who would listen to me and my woes. People were easy targets for me, as I was the hurtful kid who needed attention. No wonder I was molested by your men friends when you and Dad had parties at home.

Mom, there was so much going on in my life that you have no idea about. I never told you – I never could tell you. You would not listen to me, you just had eyes and ears for Paul.

Looking back at this time I now see how it has influenced me in the choices I made in my life. I was engaged three times but never committed to marriage or wanting kids – and that's entirely because of our relationship, or better, lack of one. And now, preferring the company of women is probably because of the emotional bond we women have and how it feels more real when we touch and share our feelings. Men want sex and women are starved for love, especially when they never experienced parental love in their childhood.

I'm not blaming you, Mom, nor Paul for the way my life has turned out. I alone am responsible for my life. It's just that not being wanted is the most difficult thing to overcome...

This chapter was about the influence you exert on others, whether you are aware of it or not. You may live your life thinking only about yourself, your priorities, your goals and objectives – and that's when you make the biggest mistake. Everything you do influences others.

So, take a quiet moment now and think about your life. Think about how you are influencing your children or loved ones, think about how their lives could be different, if YOUR blueprint were different.

Decide that it is time to discover YOUR blueprint!

However, before you undertake this journey, you need to understand a bit about the subconscious mind, as this is where your blueprint resides.

∾

Every man has in himself a continent of undiscovered character. Happy is he who acts as the Columbus to his own soul.

Sir J. Stephen

∾

Chapter 3

Why It Is So Important To Know How To Communicate With Your Subconscious Mind

The subconscious mind is mysterious to many people and yet, it is something that every single person who has ever lived on this planet has relied on to function whether or not they were aware of it. It is the deepest essence of our beings and holds the keys to everything we are and ever will be. The subconscious is our innermost self; every experience we have ever had, every thought we ever thought and every emotion we have ever experienced are held in our subconscious and have helped to form it.

The subconscious mind is the reason that some people succeed and others fail when it would appear that they are equally matched in every other way. The subconscious mind is the force that causes a hero to rush into a burning building to save a child, while another stands by crying with his head buried in his hands. This same subconscious mind causes a person to eat half a bag of cookies even though her conscious mind declared that she was on a diet.

What marks the difference between the person who ran into the burning building and the person who stood by and watched?

Did one consciously choose to become a hero and the other consciously choose to do nothing?

The difference between the actions of these two people is their subconscious programming, the blueprint. If you have ever heard an interview with a "hero" they typically all say the same thing: they weren't thinking at all; they simply reacted. The force that caused them to act was the subconscious mind. This is the same with the dieter who eats the cookies. They usually aren't thinking that they would like to sabotage their diet, they just open the bag of cookies and start eating.

The subconscious mind is a powerful force

As you can see from these examples, the subconscious mind is a powerful force that can cause a person to take action, good or bad. This is not to say that our conscious mind has no power over the subconscious, but if you are unaware of the connection and do not know how to communicate with your subconscious mind you will never gain control over it and will find yourself doomed to live the rest of your life according to your blueprint, that was programmed into you by chance.

Success in your spiritual, financial and emotional life all depends on the internal programs that exist deep within your subconscious mind. These programs tell you what your deepest held beliefs are, who and what you are, where you come from and what you are capable of accomplishing.

Hurtful words from thoughtless people in your past may have left you lacking in confidence...

Once you truly understand the power of your subconscious mind, it becomes absolutely vital that you learn how to communicate with it. Much of the programming of the subconscious mind happened as a result of chance, everything that happened in your life and every feeling you felt; but once you understand how it works you will see that the subconscious mind can be deliberately reprogrammed to help you achieve absolutely anything you want to achieve in life.

Hurtful words from thoughtless people in your past may have left you lacking in confidence and shying away from activities and behaviors you would like to have in your life; but you can learn how to cleanse these negative programs from your subconscious mind and replace them with positive thoughts which will lead you to automatically behave in a more confident manner and accept challenges you would otherwise avoid.

Taking these actions will no longer feel uncomfortable for you, in fact you won't even have to think about it at all. Like the hero who runs into the burning building, you just react in a more confident way to every stimulus around you.

How the subconscious mind works

In order to understand how the subconscious mind works, it may be helpful to contrast it with the conscious mind. There are four states of the mind, two conscious, and two subconscious:

> The conscious, or beta state, where we reason, think and solve problems in our daily waking hours

> The meditative or alpha state where brain waves slow down and it is easier to access memories and store new ones

> The theta state, the ideal state for super-learning and reprogramming your mind, dream recall and self hypnosis

> The delta, deep sleep or unconscious state

Your conscious mind is your present awareness of what you are seeing, touching, tasting, smelling and hearing. It is also the voice in your head that interprets these sensations in your internal dialogue. The data that your conscious receives from your senses, combined with the interpretation of your inner dialog and mixed with the emotions that these elements evoke are all translated and stored in your subconscious.

We are quite familiar with the conscious mind, our waking state, but generally pay little mind to the subconscious mind, which has six primary functions:

➤ It is the seat of our memories

➤ It regulates involuntary functions of the body, like breathing, digesting and controlling body temperature

➤ It is the seat of our emotions

➤ It's where our imagination comes from

➤ It controls our habits, and

➤ It provides and directs the energy that motivates us.

Your subconscious consists of memories and beliefs, the memories and beliefs that form the very core of who you are. Your subconscious may also be thought of as the link between your physical self and your inner spirit and is the means by which you can communicate with the infinite intelligence of the universe. Faith is at the core of a healthy sub-conscious and will allow it to transform any desire you have into reality.

Once you understand the inner workings of the subconscious mind, all you have to do is think about anything you wish to have or achieve and believe that it is true and the subconscious will handle the rest. The subconscious is the place where "hunches" and "feelings" (as in, "I just had a feeling that it was the right thing to do") come from. You may have heard the expression, "Let your conscience be your guide", but it is your subconscious that does most of the guiding in your life.

In fact the most powerful influences of the subconscious are due to the emotions

The subconscious has been taking in information and forming beliefs since before you were born.

Even in your mother's womb your subconscious was at work interpreting the data that was available. Although the subconscious is capable of interpreting the words you hear and your internal dialog, the information it stores is not all stored in the form of language or words.

In fact the most powerful influences of the subconscious are due to the emotions that are stored there and the way that similar external stimuli can evoke emotions from past events. For example, smelling the cologne of a former lover may instantly evoke feelings of love or remorse, depending on the emotional cues that are stored from that relationship. The smell of chocolate chip cookies baking will stimulate not only your saliva glands, but may stir up happy childhood emotions and memories as well.

The subconscious is programmed by your five senses combined with internal dialogue and emotion

I find this subject incredibly fascinating. Think of it this way: you rationalize with your logic, conscious mind that you are in a safe and secure house, you know that the alarm is on, that nobody can enter without causing it to go off, you have checked every room, looked under every bed and in every closet – you are alone and you are safe.

Yet there is the subconscious forcing itself upon you – it is braking through the rational thinking with memories of unsafe places you have been in before, your imagination goes wild conjuring up dark creatures of the night that might harm you, and then fear sets in, the kind of chilling fear that makes your heart race, your breathing shallow and your brow break out in sweat.

You survive this anxious moment today only to be triggered again tomorrow when you go and set the alarm before going to bed. Soon a habit is formed that keeps you in your imagined fear night after night, sapping up your energies that could be channeled to better and greater things.

The subconscious mind records everything like a video camera

The subconscious mind records every detail of every event that ever happened to you. It works like a video camera running day in and day out 24/7. Information is stored in your memory banks and retrieved when you want to remember something. Sometimes memories just pop up in your conscious mind and you wonder why you just thought about your sister's yellow dress or the watch you got at your high school graduation. When memories pop up like that they are generally triggered by something perceived by the five senses of your conscious mind. The more intense an event when first recorded, the faster and easier it is retrieved.

Highly charged emotional traumas such as those that trigger negative blueprints, pop up as easily as a kernel of corn on the fire. For example, if you had a traumatic experience once with a spider, it is highly likely that your subconscious mind will replay this event every time you see or hear someone talk about a spider. Your physical body would respond with anxiety, fear and racing heartbeat just like it did the first time this traumatic experience happened to you.

The subconscious mind is like a computer

Imagine the subconscious mind as a computer: all the data is stored there safely – but it takes programs to access it. These programs are your attitudes and beliefs about every aspect of your life that you formed from childhood on. Your blueprints are also such programs, whether positive or negative.

A pattern was formed in my subconscious mind that equated food with approval and love...

Here is an example of a "milder" blueprint that created a program for my view on food: I vividly remember my mother's stern voice at every meal: "Eat what's on your plate! There are starving children in China – so don't waste food!" Nothing wrong with this statement, the only problem was that I never had a say as to how much food was put on my plate.

Over the years this daily sermon became my mantra – every time I saw food I ate it, all of it and more, because food could not be wasted. I felt "bad" if I did not eat everything because that would make my mother angry and then she would withhold approval and love. A pattern was formed in my subconscious mind that equated food with approval and love, and I ended up with a lifelong weight problem.

The memory of Mom's chocolate chip cookies makes you feel good

The programs of the subconscious mind are coupled with your internal dialogue and the emotions created during your experience. In the example of the chocolate chip cookies, perhaps your first memory of this is standing on a chair in the kitchen helping your mother bake them. You probably felt proud of being able to help Mom in the kitchen when you measured and poured the ingredients in and turned on the mixer. You may have felt excited when you smelled the cookies baking. When it was finally time to eat the cookies, you had the incredible sensation of the warm melting chocolate contrasting with the simpler taste of the cookie dough and along with that you had a warm, happy feeling of spending quality time with Mom.

When you have a bad day and are overcome with the urge to bake (and eat) a couple dozen chocolate chip cookies, it is not just a "sugar buzz" you are seeking. Your subconscious mind has been programmed by your past experience that making and eating chocolate chip cookies makes you feel good.

Words are very powerful and can evoke intense emotions...

Words can evoke intense emotions

Another example of this involuntary programming is through words. Words are very powerful and can evoke intense emotions both very negative and very positive. Maybe someone in your early childhood teased you about something, perhaps they said you were stupid or ugly or slow. These words and the painful feelings they produced formed a part of your subconscious that lowered your self esteem in that area.

For instance, let's say you did poorly on a test or answered a question incorrectly in class and your classmates called you stupid. Even though it was totally natural to make a mistake and everybody does, part of you accepted the criticism that you were stupid. The effect that negative comment could have is unbelievable if it is accepted by the subconscious.

If you let that comment take root in your subconscious, that tinge of insecurity about your intelligence could stay with you throughout your life. You might shy away from books that might be too difficult (for a stupid person) to read or maybe you avoid taking the SATs because you don't want to see how stupid you really are. So, that one incorrect belief could completely change the course of your life and in some ways become a self-fulfilling prophesy because you believed you were stupid, you didn't stretch your mind and you avoided going to college, etc.

Learning to communicate with your subconscious mind gives you more power

Learning to communicate with and reprogram your subconscious mind will give you the power to create the life you have always dreamed of having. You can earn more money, enjoy better health, have more success and attract more happy and fulfilling relationships into your life. You can live in your dream house, drive any car you can imagine and attract the kind of people into your life that you want to be with. This is not fiction – it is as true as are the laws of gravity or thermo dynamics. These truths have always existed and have always worked exactly the same way whether anybody knew about or believed in them or not. These laws are no different.

The laws of the subconscious mind are always working, whether you do something about it or not. You can leave the programming of your subconscious mind to chance and accept whatever that programming creates or you can take action and learn to change the programming to create the life you want instead. You can change your blueprint!

If you were hungry and someone offered you the choice between a loaf of bread and a rock it would seem obvious that you would choose the loaf of bread. Hopefully, the choice you have between allowing the blueprint to control your life or taking the time to change that programming and have any life you choose will be just as obvious to you by the time you finish reading this book.

Whether you choose to take action or not, the words you read here will have an effect on your subconscious mind. If you choose to ignore the exercises you will solidify the belief in your subconscious mind that you are powerless to change your blueprint. If, on the other hand, you choose to follow the exercises you will be opening the door to tremendous power over your life and your future.

You have the power to reprogram your subconscious mind

The good news is that the programming of your subconscious mind does not have to be done by chance. You have the power to control a great deal of what goes into it and you can remove the negative programming. By learning to communicate with your subconscious, taking the time to be aware of the emotions you are having and by developing new thought patterns and habits, you can effectively put new information into your subconscious mind that can go to work for you to create more success, greater health and happier relationships than you have ever imagined.

There are many different methods by which you can learn how to communicate with your subconscious...

Knowing that the subconscious mind works by assimilating information that is gathered by sight, sound, touch, taste and smell and then combined with your internal dialogue and the emotions that are created, you can directly affect the information that your subconscious receives and uses to guide your life.

There are many different methods by which you can learn how to communicate with your subconscious mind. I will explain a number of these in Chapter 5 and provide additional exercises in the Appendices for you to practice this invaluable art. Also, there is a wealth of information available to you on my blog http://www. AndreaLucasBlog.com and in my articles library at http://www. AndreaLucasArticles.com. Opt in at either site and I'll deliver important information directly to your email inbox through my periodic newsletters.

Now that you have a good understanding of the power and workings of the subconscious mind, do you have the courage to face your demons?

Are you ready to take the journey from which there is no return?

What would life be if we had no courage

to attempt anything?

Vincent van Gogh

Chapter 4

Discover Your Blueprint!

In order to find your blueprint, you have to go on a little journey. You have to go back in time to when the traumatic event happened that formed your blueprint – not to relive it and bring back painful feelings, but to recognize the moment so that you can deal with it and put it to rest forever.

The process of going back in time is clinically called "regression". Regression is understood to work with the mind and psyche. Frequently a state of regression is achieved through hypnosis, but it can just as easily be achieved by entering into a state of deep relaxation. I prefer the latter method because this way you remain conscious of everything that is happening and you can make choices along the way and participate in the discovery process.

Learn how to meditate

Meditation is a wonderful way to relax the mind. I know, because I learned to meditate. It's easy, everyone can do it, and once you get the hang of it – you'll love it!

The mind races at 50-60,000 thoughts per day. It has no "off button". Even at night, the mind keeps going and produces the most wonderful – and sometimes horrible – dreams. When pleasant thoughts cross your mind, you automatically relax, all tension leaves your body and you feel great. After a pleasant dream you wake up refreshed and ready to take on the world.

When something is bothering you, however, your thoughts become a prison – anytime you try to break out of it, the confining thoughts pop up again like barbed wire, keeping you confined to dwell on them. Your body tenses up and physical pain is added to the emotional pain that you are trying to rid yourself of. Meditation helps to break this vicious cycle.

When something is bothering you... your thoughts become a prison...

Meditation is an ancient art, which has been practiced for thousands of years in Asia. What used to invoke images of Buddhist monks in crimson robes, sitting in deep trance in the lotus position, has now become commonplace in our world. I was at an upscale restaurant the other day when I noticed a young man sitting with his legs lotus-like entwined while chatting animatedly with his lady companion. Hardly anyone else noticed or found it strange enough to comment on. Meditation is taught today as part of yoga classes, in karate training, in medical centers for stress reduction and is practiced by star athletes to prepare themselves for competition.

The act of meditation involves both inward contemplation of an object as well as complete absorption in it through concentrating on it. When we concentrate on one thing – an object, a sound, a thought – we do so at the exclusion of all other thoughts. Meditation functions therefore to transform our consciousness.

I like to meditate by looking into the blue and yellow flame of an ordinary wax candle. I choose my favorite room in the house, a quiet place, sheltered from outside noises, and I close the door, lower the window shades and turn off all electric lights. Only the candle burns. I cannot manage the lotus position, nor am I comfortable sitting cross-legged on the floor, so I select an easy chair, put on soft classical music, and take a deep breath to physically prepare my body for the process of mental relaxation.

I begin by gazing into the flame just inches in front of me on the coffee table. At first my eyes focus on the flame and I pay attention to the flickering, the rise and fall of the blue hue at the wick of the candle and the haze caused by the heated air above the flame. I notice the flame change shape with the movement of the air around it – it dilates, extends to twice its height with the tip reaching high up into the air, then retracts, becomes almost round, and then repeats its mesmerizing dance in the darkened room.

As my eyes become less focused on the flame, I notice the halo, like a yellow golden aura around the flame. And soon, as I become more relaxed, my eyelids close a bit, and my focus shifts away from the flame – I no longer look at it, but through it. Now everything in my vision becomes softer, fuzzier and the halo, the aura around the flame gets bigger, bluer and now envelopes the entire candle. All the while my mind is blank – I think of nothing. And this is what meditation is all about, to quiet the mind.

Learning the basics of relaxation techniques is not difficult, but it does require repeated practice. I suggest you check out the exercises in Appendix B for a variety of choices on relaxation methods and pick one for this session.

Regression is your best vehicle

In regression you don't want to think – you want to feel and do or say what you really want. When you go back in time and reach the critical moment of your blueprint's creation, you have a choice of changing that moment by changing your perception of it. Remember, when this moment happened you were a small child with underdeveloped cognitive skills and you could not rationalize like you can today.

If you recall from my experience, I formed an opinion of the world and my place in it based on one single traumatic event. I did not analyze the situation – I just felt my world fall apart and then interpreted this feeling in my subconscious mind as an irrefutable fact that from that moment on became my reality – my blueprint.

Now, when you regress, you can confront your tormentor – be it a bully, an abusive parent, a thoughtless teacher; you also can confront an animal that scared you – like a vicious dog, a spider that bit you or a squid that stung you; you can even confront an event that happened, such as an accident that took the lives of your parents or an illness that crippled you or a loved one. The purpose of the confrontation is to allow you to express your feelings about the situation in a way you could not express when you were a small child.

However, in this part of the exercise we will not work on the confrontation part. We will work on that in Chapter 5. For now, I just want you to go back in time and recognize the moment that created your blueprint. So, let's begin!

Go back in time

I challenge you now to take a look at your life.

> First, use your conscious mind to go back to when you were a young child. Think about the events that you can remember easily, and write them down, any event, birthday party, splash in a summer pool, sitting on Grandma's lap, riding the bicycle for the first time, anything that
>
>
>
> comes to mind easily. Then reflect on that list and go back to each event and picture it clearly in your mind – how did you feel? Was it a happy or sad moment? Did you feel good, or angry or fearful? Why does this moment stay with you out of the million memories you have had since childhood? Who

was with you at that moment? A parent, sibling, teacher, stranger? What was their role in this event? What were the words they said to you, the actions they took, the non-verbal communication that clearly entered your mind, your being, to be imprinted there forever?

Work on this list of events for a while until you are able to visualize these events clearly in your mind's eye. Be aware as you are going through this exercise, that finding your blueprint can be a very emotional journey.

You may want to have a loved one by your side to help you through this process, to hold your hand or lend a shoulder to cry on. In fact, a friend or relative (I'll call them your guide) would be very helpful in leading you through the process of relaxation. If you want, you could seek the services of a hypnotist, but as I said this is not necessary at this time.

➤ Brief your guide on what you are about to do and why, and ask them to go on this journey of discovery with you. Together read the methods on relaxation and visualization outlined in the accompanying Appendices and select one you want to use for this session.

➤ When you are ready, prepare yourself physically for the experience. Wear comfortable clothes, remove your shoes and relax in a reclining chair or on the bed. Draw the window shades or turn down the lights in the room to create a soothing environment. Turn off the TV and play relaxing classical or new age background music if you like.

➤ Allow your guide to lead you through your chosen relaxation method now and bring you gently and safely to a state of deep relaxation. Remember, you will be completely aware of everything that happens. This is important because you will use your recollections later on when you are ready to process them and write your new blueprint.

When you are completely relaxed, the regression session can begin.

➤ Your guide will now begin to count you back through the years. The task of finding the critical event is actually given to the subconscious mind and your guide is just the conduit.

➤ Let your mind go where it wants to go, do not try to consciously guide it. Do not be concerned when your guide asks you to go back to a time when you were, say, 10 years old and you "see" nothing in your mind. Try again. Resistance is normal at first until you become comfortable with the questioning and you find your voice.

➤ Let your guide probe you again with another question, and another until you respond – when you recall a moment/event in your life like a replay of a movie that you have seen before. Perhaps you see yourself at the school playground, or in your Mom's kitchen or going for a walk with your dog.

When you see these first pictures replay in your mind, you will know instinctively where you are and how old you are. And you will know whether this picture brings up emotions, positive or negative. Your guide will also notice your reaction – and either move on to prompt you to recall another event, or linger on this one if it seems to have evoked negative emotions.

➤ Go through this process of revisiting past events until you both realize that you have come upon the core event that was responsible for your blueprint. Your mind will take you to the specific point in time you need to revisit right now.

When you recognize this crucial event, I want you to concentrate on your feelings. Your guide will ask you now four questions:

1. How do you feel?

Describe your emotions – say anything that comes to your mind and ask your guide to write it down. Let go completely, cry if you want, and capture every emotion you feel. You know that you are just observing an old incident and that you are in no danger now. Yet you can feel the emotions your younger self felt at that time and that makes you present in the moment.

Your answer might be "I'm angry" or "I'm scared" or "I'm sad", or "I feel hurt" (not because of physical but emotional pain). Most likely it will be one of these core emotions that you are able to express when you are speaking with your child's voice.

2. How do you feel about people?

This question does not address the actual people that were present at the crucial event, but people in general. If someone hurt you in the past and your answer to Question 1 above was "I'm scared" your answer might be: "People are hurtful – they are out to get me" or "People are unkind". If the answer was "I am angry", your answer now might be: "People are infuriating" or "People cannot be trusted". And if you said "I'm sad" before, you might say now: "People will leave me" or "People are not nice, they don't like me".

3. How do you feel about the world?

When you are angry, scared or sad and think people are unkind and cannot be trusted – how do you feel about the world then? Do these feelings extend to everyone in the world? Is the world a good place to live in and raise your children? Is the world safe or is it dangerous? And lastly,

4. How do you feel about the future?

Do you see a glorious and wonderful future for yourself, or do you see pain, uncertainty, danger? Do you see love and happiness in your future, or do you feel that you will be unloved and banished to a life of loneliness?

These are of course just some guidelines so you know how to answer these questions. Use your own words – let your emotions find the right words for you! As you wish, you may linger in the moment, recollect the event in all its details, listen again to what was said to you or about you, look at the faces of the people who were present.

Listen to other sounds in the room or place where you are at, look around you to perhaps discover something that had escaped you earlier that might shed a different light on your experience now and explore all of your emotions. When you do this you open up your conscious and subconscious minds to the possibility of reconciliation in the confrontation phase, which is discussed in Chapter 5.

When you are ready, your guide will bring you now back to your full wakeful state, if you are not there already. At this point, your reaction to your discovery could be highly emotional and physically painful, as it was in my case, or one of complete surprise. Like what happened with my son Paul – his reaction was: "You mean to say it's that simple? That is the reason for my issues...?"

For him the moment of my leaving was not a hidden memory that had been suppressed and had to be brought back into his conscious mind through regression. No, it was there all along, he just did not recognize it as the event that triggered his blueprint.

When I discovered my blueprint, the emotional impact of the discovery that the direction of my life was formed sixty years ago had a shock effect on my body. Within minutes I had a migraine headache (I never have headaches). I was shivering like with high fever, and unstoppable tears were streaming down my face. These were tears of release, release from the burdens that I have been carrying on my shoulders, in my heart and in my soul.

Whether your reaction mimics mine or simply changes your perception of the event now that you know about its relevance to your blueprint, you will need to deal with the new realities in your life. After all, when putting it altogether, and using my examples above...

> ➤ if you feel angry; and people cannot be trusted; and the world is like quicksand, where you had to be on alert all

the time so as not to fall into it and die; and therefore your future is grim, gloomy and nothing to look forward to…

or…

> if you feel scared; and people are out to get you; and the world is dangerous; and therefore your future is miserable and hopeless…

or…

> if you feel sad; and people will leave you; and the world is a lonely and uninviting place; and therefore your future is depressing and despondent…

then… how can you possibly be happy and enjoy your life?

Finding your blueprint and clearing your mind of it will bring you joy, unbelievable joy and a new perspective on life. You will be strong, and powerful and ready to make the next chapter in your life a happy and incredibly fulfilled one – I promise!

Here is what Ingrid T. from Phoenix, AZ had to say after she discovered her blueprint:

I was absolutely terrified when I first started this process. I had no idea what I was going to get into, and I was scared. I could not imagine what I could possibly discover during this session. I asked a friend of mine to be my guide - she has had some experience with hypnosis before, so it was not that scary for her.

At first, I could not see anything when she asked me to tell her where I was when I was six years old; but then all of a sudden I remembered the scene when I was holding on to my Dad's legs as we were climbing up the mountain. Actually, it was just a small hill about a minute behind our house. Dad was holding on to me, and then all of a sudden he slipped and he fell, and I fell and we both rolled down the hill. I was scared and hurt – and now I know that that was the moment when I decided that I could not rely on my Dad to protect me.

All these years, when my Dad did something for me, I did not trust him. I did not take his advice in anything, not when he was talking to me about college, or dating or choice of profession. I am so grateful for the insight I have received from your course and instructions on regression theory that allowed me to realize the big mistake I made based on my blueprint. I talked with my Dad and we are both glad to be friends again thanks to you!

I got this letter from John S. from Chicago, IL, after he took the journey of discovery:

Andrea, I cannot begin to tell you what difference your guidance has made in my life. My wife has been on my case for years for starting one project after the other but never finishing one. I've been to photography school for two years and quit just before graduation; I've taken flying lessons, soloed a few times, and then quit before taking the final test; I've enjoyed scuba diving all my life and decided I wanted to become a certified instructor – I was the best in my class – but I quit just before I became certified. No matter what I started, I never finished it.

When I followed your instructions and had my Dad lead me through the regression session, he (or should I say – my subconscious mind) brought me to the day my grandmother died. I loved her dearly and I was crushed when she died. I was no more than seven years old. I had been helping her weeding her garden that day when she felt ill all of a sudden. She sat down on the grass, looked at me and said: "Oh, I should not have finished it" – and then she died (of a heart attack, as I later found out).

Now I know that these last words of my beloved grandmother formed the blueprint in my subconscious mind that warned me – when you finish something you'll surely die! No wonder I never finished what I started. Thank you, Andrea, for opening my eyes and allowing me to live again without this irrational fear!

And Susan S. from Seattle, Washington wrote this about her experience when she discovered her blueprint:

I did not have a relative or friend whom I could trust to lead me through the process of discovery, so I decided to trust in my own ability. I used your example of the candle light meditation and the strangest thing happened to me: as I was looking into the flame and watching it dance up and down, all of a sudden I saw my mother's stern face staring at me through the blue hue of the flame.

I saw her clearly, with the familiar disapproving look on her face as if she was saying – what foolishness are you up to now? Don't you have anything better to do? In this weird and wonderful place I found myself in at this moment, it came to me that my mother never once had said a word of praise to me. And this made me realize why I had so little joy in my life, why I could not feel happy about my accomplishments and never believed when anyone else had something positive to say about me or my work.

Well, Andrea, this ends right now! You have shown me that I am worthy and I thank you for opening my eyes and heart to the possibilities that await me in my life now.

There is only one person who could ever make you happy, and that person is you.

David Burns, Intimate Connections

Chapter 5

How To Deal With The Emotional Stress Of Discovery

How To Communicate With Your Subconscious Mind
To Successfully Erase Your Old Blueprint

N ow that you have discovered your blueprint – you might be frustrated and angry, very angry. Perhaps you think that you have wasted many years and that your life could have been so much better, much more rewarding and fulfilling, if only you had lived by a different blueprint…

Perhaps you need a punching bag to release your anger, or perhaps you want to shut yourself off completely from the world and speak with no one. Sooner or later though, you will find the need to deal with the emotional stress of discovery, so that you can move on, create your new blueprint and live a happy and fulfilled life.

One of the most important things for you to know is that the effects of a negative blueprint do not have to be permanent. What happened to you in your childhood does not need to ruin the rest of your life! Equally important, you also do not need to spend the rest of your life relying on support groups or medications, or being in therapy or counseling. While such methods can indeed be of short-term help, they can also create dependency. The bottom line is they can keep you stuck – living in the problem rather than in the solution.

Live in the solution – not the problem

A traumatic experience impacts a person. If the trauma was ongoing, the effects are usually more severe; but even one experience can create immeasurable damage.

Whether your childhood trauma was a matter of witnessing a horrible event, or, as occurs even more often, being on the receiving-end of physical, sexual, or extreme emotional abuse, you have probably already experienced plenty of consequences from it.

As we have seen from the numerous celebrities who have come forth with their stories, childhood trauma often leads to a host of problems. These can include eating disorders, substance abuse, inability to form and maintain healthy relationships, and many other difficulties. These problems themselves can lead a trauma survivor to feeling helpless and hopeless.

Living in the solution means addressing the cause of these problems at its source. When you can face the trauma and acknowledge it for what it was, you are making progress toward the solution. When you work through all of those feelings of pain, anger, and confusion, you are taking the best steps toward letting them go.

Living in the solution means addressing the cause of these problems at its source.

If you experienced trauma in your childhood, I hope that you are now at a turning point. You may be ready to acknowledge exactly how damaging those experiences eventually became to you – the impact they had on virtually every area of your life. If you are also ready to make some positive changes and begin living in the solution rather than existing in the problem, you are now opening the door to a brighter and happier future.

Put the past behind you!

Are you ready to put the past in the past – and finally be free of its effects? Do not create further dependency – whether keeping the old problem or adding new ones, doing so is not the answer. Find answers that are not only much more positive but also much better in the long run. The very best answer of all is that your life can finally be in your own hands, to live and experience as you wish! This can all be yours – as soon as you begin living in the solution!

There are a number of techniques available to you that will help you live in the solution and overcome the negative feelings of frustration, anger and perhaps even rage. I have used them all and strongly suggest to you and urge you to do the same. Your recovery process will be easier and much faster than if you do nothing. Yes, time heals all wounds, but why extend the pain when there are wonderful and effective ways to shorten the suffering?

During your recovery process you are not only learning to manage your negative emotions, you are laying the foundations for your New Blueprint, which I will discuss in the next chapter. You are creating your new reality which should be based on forgiveness, internal peace and love.

The tasks I am assigning you here will help you achieve these positive feelings and lead you to the abundant life you are yearning for – so don't skip any of them!

Seek support from family, friends and support groups

When I needed love and support to help me work through my emotions, I was blessed with the presence of two of my life coaches, Jase Souder (http://www.lifetigers.com) and Harold Maloy (http://www.haroldmaloy.com), who were at my side as I fell apart both emotionally and physically. Their expertise and unconditional love helped me through the recovery process. If you have friends and relatives who could be there for you at this trying time, call on

them to help you. Try to identify a few key people you can talk to openly, tell them and ask them anything.

Emotional support involves understanding, patience, affection and encouragement. Your support systems involve the people, organizations and activities that are there to help you deal with the emotions you are experiencing and offer you encouragement and comfort during difficult times. Emotional support systems might include family, friends, co-workers, neighbors, and support groups. There could be many or just a few of them who come to your help in times of need.

If you do have an emotional support group, think about how you would like to communicate with them. Would an occasional phone call suffice, or would you prefer daily talks over a cup of coffee? Would you prefer structured counseling, or ad-hoc walks in the park to get some fresh air while clearing your mind of pent-up feelings? What are you comfortable with?

Make your decision and let your support group know what you prefer. Keeping the lines of communication open is very important here, as nobody wants to guess and then find that they have caused you more grief instead of having helped.

Be mindful of the fact that your emotional support system might change over time.

Be mindful of the fact that your emotional support system might change over time. You may find that close friends become more distant as they realize their own limitations or issues when helping you with your emotional state – or, you may find that distant acquaintances become close friends, as they become intuned with your story. Either way, be grateful for their support and thank them for being there for you.

Learn how to meditate

I have already covered one form of meditation in the previous chapter. There are many ways to meditate. In addition to my favorite way to meditate with a candle, I have included others in Appendix B.

When you practice meditation often, you will find that your self-interest and self-concern will change. Instead of dwelling on your blueprint and all the negativity associated with it, you will uncover inner resources of compassion and wisdom that will help you overcome obstacles and act in beneficial ways towards others as well. These activities will reduce your suffering, and the process will become effortless through the simple practice of meditation.

Study hypnosis and self hypnosis

If you are like most people, you probably have a little knowledge about the subject of hypnosis. Unfortunately, if you are like most people, what you know is probably based on numerous misconceptions. While popular opinion about hypnosis generally revolves around fun, foolishness, or danger, there is a much more positive aspect of hypnosis which fewer people know about – and you should hear about it, because it has the potential to cause many positive changes in your life!

In many instances, your own mind is your best ally and your best defense.

What hypnosis can do for you

When your mind is approached by the method of hypnosis, there are nearly-limitless possibilities for what it can do for you! One of the most wonderful benefits of hypnosis is that it can greatly assist in ridding you of certain types of personal difficulties. If you have tried every other method to quit smoking cigarettes, using alcohol, drugs, or other addictions which are psychological as well as physical, or if you have been apprehensive about trying any method at all for fear that nothing would work as well as you needed, hypnosis can be the answer you have been seeking. And, of course, hypnosis is a wonderful way of ridding yourself of the effects of your old blueprint!

You may be one of the many who suffer from insomnia. If so, you are aware of all of the negative repercussions one can suffer as a result of consistent lack of sleep. You probably know that insomnia has a horrible effect on your ability to think clearly and function properly in everyday life. Insomnia, and all of the difficulties associated with it, need not be a part of your life – hypnosis can be your aid in attaining healthful, restful sleep!

If you have trouble with your memory, depression, self-esteem issues, and other psychologically-based problems, you do not have to resign yourself to spending the rest of your life suffering from such problems, or putting years or decades into therapy, or relying on medications. In many instances, your own mind is your best ally and your best defense. You can begin to feel almost like an entirely new person, with a brand-new healthy lease on life, when your difficulties are addressed and resolved through hypnosis!

You have already been hypnotized

Have you ever been totally absorbed while reading a book or watching a movie? When I get engrossed in the plot, all thoughts and worries about my job and my family fade away. I'm so mesmerized by the action on the screen that I don't notice what's going on around me. Has this happened to you? If so, you've experienced a mental state that's similar to what happens to you during hypnosis.

Hypnosis is simply a technique by which one person (the hypnotist) gives suggestions to another person (the subject), and the subject believes these suggestions and acts upon them. There is no hocus-pocus involved at all. If you have ever watched a commercial and then went out to buy the product advertised – you have been hypnotized. Millions of dollars are spent every year by large corporations developing 30 second commercials to be aired during the Super Bowl. They know that millions of people will be watching the game, and that most of them will be "mesmerized" watching the event – and the commercials – intently, and thus be in a highly suggestible state.

You can easily see how we are controlled by our subconscious mind and how important it is to find ways to communicate with it. Both meditation and hypnosis are excellent conduits to the subconscious mind. Like meditation, hypnosis creates a state of deep relaxation and quiets the mind, only much more intense and with the intent of bringing about changes in emotions or behavior. When you are hypnotized, your attention is more focused and you are more open to suggestions. You feel uninhibited and relaxed because you tune out the worries and doubts that normally keep your actions in check.

Both meditation and hypnosis are excellent conduits to the subconscious mind.

The Rules of the Mind

So how can you bring about desired changes in emotions and/or behavior through hypnosis? Let's examine the Rules of The Mind, as identified by the late Charles Tebbets, "the Grandmaster of Hypnotherapy":

1. ***Every thought or idea causes a physical reaction.*** The subconscious mind reacts to strong emotional events (thoughts or ideas) because that is where our feelings reside. A negative event that produces anxiety or fear once will always produce anxiety and fear the next time it happens again. To rid ourselves of this negative event, we must open the doors to our subconscious (through hypnosis or other means) and change or eliminate that event from our memory banks.

2. ***What's expected tends to be realized.*** In other words, what we think is what we become. The brain responds to mental images and the subconscious mind acts to materialize these mental images, which are the blueprint of a person's life. As you know from my blueprint, I held

images of men's and women's roles in my mind and my subconscious mind interpreted all of my actions and beliefs in such a way as to validate my blueprint. Keeping positive images in mind is the key to positive experiences in life, and hypnosis is a means of replacing negative images with positive ones.

3. *Imagination is more powerful than knowledge when dealing with the mind.* As we have seen above, imagination can overshadow any rational thought, especially when strong emotions are involved, like fear, anger, hatred and love. We must reach deep into the subconscious mind to remove old events and replace them with new images, which is effectively done through hypnosis.

4. *Opposing ideas cannot be held at the same time.* This is a simple but often misused concept. Like no two people can be physically in the same space, two opposing ideas – like good and bad, or honest and dishonest – cannot be held in the mind at the same time. For example, preaching to others about the transgression of stealing while pocketing change from the offering receptacle at church will only cause conflict in the mind and potentially physical discomfort or pain in the body. To achieve peace of mind, opposing ideas must be eliminated, again through hypnosis or other therapeutic methods.

5. *Once an idea has been accepted by the subconscious mind, it remains until it is replaced by another idea.* This rule of the mind has held me captive for six decades, since there was no replacement available. The habit of thinking in accordance with my blueprint was formed early on, and the longer that habit was held, the stronger it became. It took all of the steps discussed in this book, including meditation, body work and hypnosis to change my blueprint.

6. *An emotionally induced symptom tends to cause organic change if persisted in long enough.* As discussed earlier, the

child that is told by its parents consistently that it is a "pain in the neck" will in fact develop a pain in the neck such as muscle cramping, spinal problems, even cancer, later on in life if it believes this statement to be true on an emotional level, and allows its subconscious to repeat it over and over again. We are mind and body and the two cannot be separated. When hypnosis eliminates the thought of the pain, the pain itself could vanish also unless serious bodily deterioration has already taken place.

7. *Each suggestion acted upon creates less opposition to successive suggestion.* Like children learn to speak through repetition, so does the subconscious mind require repetition. All suggestions through any means of communication must be repeated over and over again to have the desired effect. Practice makes perfect.

8. *When dealing with the subconscious mind and its functions, the greater the conscious effort, the less the subconscious response.* Try not to force changes on to the subconscious mind, as it will not respond. Instead, develop positive mental images of how you would like your life to be, and reinforce these images in your subconscious mind through meditation, self hypnosis, affirmations and visualization. The results will be miraculous and lead to a more relaxed, healthier and more fulfilling life.

My hypnosis session with Jase Souder

Enough of the theory. Let me show you what happened in my hypnosis session with Jase Souder, a highly skilled hypnotist and Founder of Life Tigers, LLC. Life Tigers (http://www.lifetigers.com) is a powerful personal development program that has taught thousands of students to create their dream lives.

Jase and I agreed before our session that we would not revisit the moment my blueprint was formed, so as not to induce rebounding emotions, but to instead work on my old feelings of unworthiness and being a bad girl.

"Andrea", Jase says in a low voice, "make yourself comfortable, relax your body and mind, and let's begin."

Jase talks me through a series of relaxation suggestions to make my body limp and loose and to calm my conscious mind, so that he can more readily access my subconscious mind where the seat of my memories are located. I follow his hypnotic suggestions willingly and go into a deep, relaxing state of wakefulness. I know where I am and that Jase is here. I feel no pressure, no anxiety; my body feels very heavy and weightless at the same time. My eyes are closed and I listen to Jase's voice:

"Andrea, I want you to go back in time when you were a little girl. Can you do this?" I nod. "Ok, tell me where you are". "I'm in our living room, in Vienna where I grew up." "Good," says Jase, "are you alone?" "No, everyone is at home." "Who's that?" "My Mom, my sister, my brother – and Herr Biel" "That's your mother's friend, isn't he?" "Yes, I don't like him", I say. "Why not?" "He stinks, and he has yellow fingers and teeth" I say in my child's voice, which by now has taken on a tremor of fear.

"Are you scared?" asks Jase. "Yes, I'm hiding under the table so no one can see me." "Why are you hiding?" "Because it's Krampus Day and I don't like it". I get agitated now, remembering, being there when Herr Biel pulls me out from under the table and drags me to the door to face this horrible creature. Jase senses my discomfort and prompts me to skip this scene.

"Andrea", he says, "you are safe now. Krampus has gone away and so has Herr Biel. You are in your bed now and you are warm and comfortable under your covers. I know you were scared then when you were little. Tell me, Andrea, what would you like to tell little Andrea, now that you are all grown up?"

I blink. I am back in my adult self and I say: "I would tell little Andrea that she is a good girl, that she does not need to be afraid, that she did nothing wrong." "OK, talk to her then" says Jase. "Andrea," I say, as tears are streaming down my face, "you are good, no matter what they say, you are a *good girl and I love you". Little Andrea responds in Jase's voice: "No, I'm a bad girl – Krampus came to take me with him and I peed in my panties". "Why do you think you are bad?" I ask. Jase changes roles – "You answer her" he says.*

And so I engage in a dialog with my younger self, telling my older self from my child perspective how the memories of that awful day had convinced me that I was bad and that I had to be punished. From my older perspective I tell her about adults and how they were wrong in what they did to her on Krampus day. I tell her that she was loved and that they never thought that she was wicked.

Little Andrea wants to convince me that she was bad because she did not listen to her mother, that she had taken her brother's toys, and so on. And I tell her that she had made a mistake but that that does not make her a bad girl – and so we speak to each other for a while. I alternate crying as my younger self, who is relieved of the burden of believing that I am bad and have to be punished, and as my older self, who is full of sorrow for the lifetime spent putting myself down and punishing myself.

When we are spent crying, Jase takes my hands and says: "Andrea, little Andrea is right here in front of you – embrace her with all your heart" – and so I do. My two selves merge into one and at that moment my soul is at peace.

I have forgiven myself for whatever I did or thought I had done, I have forgiven the adults for making me believe I was to blame, and I have forgiven myself for not recognizing my true glorious self before today.

My hypnotic session with Jase has forever freed me of the burden I carried with me for six decades – thank you Jase!

Whether you seek out an experienced hypnotist or wish to use auto-suggestions you will find that the practices of hypnosis and meditation can be life altering techniques that can help you rid yourself of limiting beliefs, phobias and old blueprints.

Hypnosis is an excellent tool to combat a variety of deep rooted physical and psychological problems, such as obesity, lack of self esteem, lack of fulfillment, anxieties, phobias, fears, sexual frustration and dysfunction and others.

It is through this technique that you can confront your enemies, your tormentors that were the cause of the creation of your blueprint. In your hypnosis session you can speak with them, ask them why they did what they did and get to hear their side of the story. If you are lucky, they will see how they wronged you and ask for forgiveness. If not, you can forgive them anyway and put the trauma behind for good.

It is through this technique that you can confront your enemies, your tormentors...

Seek out a bodywork specialist

The National Institute of Health noted in a 2004 press release that more than one third of US adults use complementary and alternative medicine in addition to conventional medicine when they are faced with medical and emotional issues. The most common forms of such complementary and alternative medical therapies are chiropractic care, yoga, massage and bodywork.

Bodywork is a term used to describe any therapeutic, healing or personal development work which involves some form of touching, energy work, or the physical manipulation of the body. Bodywork includes all forms of massage techniques (there are over 80 of them), including those that allow the patients to enhance their awareness of the body-mind connection.

Anyone who has ever had a good massage knows that it feels great and relaxes the body. But this type of massage has only a temporary effect, a short term release of muscle tension, which does little to release emotional tension and stress. Once a week I get a massage by a trained and experienced massage therapist at my chiropractor's office. His job is to find the knots in my back that were caused by stress of a week's work in the office, and then to work on my muscles until all tension is gone. I feel great for a few days and then tension builds up again and I need another massage... a never-ending cycle.

Bodywork differs greatly from a muscle massage. Instead of looking for cramped muscle tissue, the practitioner searches for spots in the body where pent-up emotions are blocking the energy flow. Energy must flow freely for the body to be healthy, balanced and harmonized. Any negative emotion that is not resolved, such as fear, anger and depression, leaves a scar on the psyche that is physically manifested in form of an energy blockage in the body.

The physical place where such a blockage appears can be anywhere in the body, but is most often found in the abdominal region where soft tissue is located. Pain may, or may not be present in the location of the blockage, which is often detected only by the skillful probing of the practitioner's hands. When a blockage is found and manipulated, strange and wonderful things happen to both the body and the soul of the patient.

Memory of negative emotions is stored in body tissue the same way as physical pain. When you are near the place, object or person that hurt you physically or emotionally, your body remembers and cramps up with fear. You anticipate being hurt again and muster up all defenses to avoid the pain, whether physical or emotional. If physical, you protect your body as good as you can or you run away. If emotional, you shut out feelings, close yourself off and allow nothing to get to you, not even love. Bodywork removes the bad memories by removing the energy blockages in the body and retrains the tissue to feel good again, the way it did before the hurt.

My bodywork session with Harold Maloy

Here is what happened to me when Harold Maloy, Founder of The Maloy Method of Healing (http://www.haroldmaloy.com) worked on me for the first time:

I am stretched out on the sofa and Harold is sitting close by. He talks me though deep relaxation exercises and uses a bit of hypnosis to completely relax me. I trust him totally and know that he will not harm me in any way. I feel his hands on my clothed body now, his fingers dancing, probing along the edges of my pelvis, up the right side of my body, over the liver, the stomach, up to my sternum, and down the other side, the spleen, the ascending colon and over the small intestines across the whole pelvis area. Here and there his fingers stop, pressure mounts and a scream escapes my lips – where does this pain come from?

Harold's fingers work on this spot while his words are soothing and comforting until I am completely relaxed again. He speaks to me of love, of forgiveness and faith, not in a religious but universal sense. Believe in yourself, he says, you are not a victim, you are strong, you are powerful, you are loved – and I believe him.

The dancing fingers move on, probe some more and then come back to the same spot – now I feel no more pain. I feel release, I feel like moving my body, I feel like dancing – I laugh and I cry. I feel light in body, mind and spirit and I enjoy the emotion of peace, security and well-being.

When our session is over, I feel a wonderful glowing radiance flowing through me and around me. There is a sparkle in my eyes and happiness in my soul that promises to remain with me forever.

Use affirmations to communicate with your subconscious mind

As you now know, the subconscious mind is much more powerful than the conscious mind, which is limited to input from our five physical senses – sight, hearing, touch, smell and taste. Aside from having total control over your physical body and all its functions and sensations, the subconscious mind influences the conscious mind through the set of rules and beliefs that are anchored in it.

These rules are established through the blueprint as well as other repetitive behavior. So, you must find a way to communicate with your subconscious mind to change the old blueprint to your new one.

Affirmations are an excellent way to communicate with your subconscious mind. When you are affirming something repeatedly, either out loud or silently speaking to yourself, you are creating a new belief – which is much like forming a new habit. If you want to break a bad habit, say eating junk food in front of the television, you set yourself a new regimen that forces you to eat only while sitting at the kitchen or dining room table.

You do this every day until the new habit is formed and you no longer think about food while watching your favorite shows. The new habit has forced out the old one – and it works just like that with your subconscious mind. Talk to it daily, repeat your affirmations over and over again, and soon your old limiting beliefs will be pushed away by the new beliefs which you now hold.

I use the following affirmations that define who I am today: "I am whole, perfect, strong, powerful, loving, harmonious, grateful and happy"

> **Whole** – because I am complete in every way, nothing is missing

> **Perfect** – because my body, mind and soul are perfect as they are

> **Strong** – because I am whole and perfect and thus strong

> **Powerful** – because my inner strength gives me the power to achieve everything I want in life

> **Loving** – because I attain to achieve the highest emotion of love

> **Harmonious** – because I am at peace with the world and everyone in it

> **Grateful** – because my past, present and future experiences bring me closer to my higher power, and

> **Happy** – because happiness is a blissful state of being

Every day when I wake up, the first things that enter my mind are these affirmations. I repeat them ten-twenty times while still lingering in bed. I repeat them while in the shower, while driving to work, anytime I find myself drifting and especially, every time I feel a negative thought entering my mind. And again at night just before I go to sleep, I repeat my personal affirmations ten-twenty times. Altogether I might say them a hundred times a day or more.

Write your own affirmations – or use mine, but start talking to your subconscious mind now! Take a look at Appendix D for a number of suggestions of affirmations that might suit you. Try this for a month and see your energy shift, notice how much better you feel, observe your happy disposition and become aware of all the other positive changes in your life! You will be amazed...

Practice visualization

Visualization is just another name for imagination. As children we were experts in this subject. Not drawing on personal experiences like we do as adults, children use their minds to create images. Long before the first film of the Harry Potter series hit the theaters, every child I know that had read the books was able to describe to me in great detail the moving staircases of Hogwarts Castle, the floating ghosts that live there, the talking pictures on the walls and the excitement of a fast Quiddich game – all in intricate detail retold from the images in their minds.

As we grow older and accumulate personal experiences, we tend to draw on these experiences instead of using our imagination – and thus we often lose part of our early ability to visualize. Visualization imprints images on your mind and they are an important means of communication with your subconscious. The more vivid your imagination (your visualization) is, the stronger the message to your subconscious and to the Universe.

The power of visualization is confirmed by science!

Many experiments have been conducted on the power of visualization, for example, this one was done at the University of Chicago:

students of like ability in playing basketball were divided into three groups and told to practice foul shots. Their scores were recorded for comparison with scores after the experiment. The first group of students was told to practice shooting foul shots for one hour each day for 30 days. The second group was told not to play basketball at all for the next 30 days and the third group was told to imagine playing basketball and to shoot foul shots only in their minds.

At the end of the 30 days the test was repeated and the scores were compared. Performance improvements were stunning: of course, the group that stopped playing altogether did not improve. However, the group that imagined shooting foul shots in their minds had improved as much as the group that actually practiced!

This is so because the subconscious mind does not distinguish between an actual event and an imagined one.

Visualization is actually quite simple to do. In fact, you probably do it all the time without realizing it. When I drive home at night from work and contemplate about what I'm going to cook for dinner, I "look" into the fridge and pantry to "see" what's there. In my mind's eye, I see the spinach and veggies in the bottom drawer of the fridge, "ah, that will make a great salad!" I think.

A quick "look" to the side door of the fridge confirms that there is vinaigrette dressing, so no need to stop at the grocery store. I "see" what's in the fridge, clear enough to know that making dinner will be a cinch. And I don't stop there – my imagination paints the entire evening in vivid colors: the dinner table, my family around me, relaxing around the fireplace, perhaps watching a movie or reading a book.

...the subconscious mind does not distinguish between an actual event and an imagined one.

Does this ring a bell with you? If you can imagine your own living room, you know how to visualize. If I ask you to think about shopping, where do you "see" yourself? Is it a department store at the Mall where you are trying on a new pair of shoes, or are you standing in line at the grocery store waiting your turn to pay? Something surely popped into your mind, as the mind unfailingly produces a picture.

Everything man-made has been first visualized in someone's mind

Look around you – everything you see that is man-made, has first been visualized – created – in someone's mind. Thought has produced the image as well as the way to make, construct the item imagined. Everything – from the pen I use to write with, to the paper I am writing on, the chair I sit in, the house I live in, the car I drive – simply everything was first seen, visualized, in someone's mind.

So, start thinking about what you want! Concentrate on one thing at a time and imagine it in as much detail as you possibly can. If it's a thing you want like a new car, picture it clearly, the make and model you want, its color and how the new leather will smell and how you will feel when you are driving it. If it's a new job you want, see yourself in it, doing the work and loving it. And a new relationship – imagine your dream partner, the way he/she looks, how compatible you are and how much you enjoy your time together.

Visualizing your dreams creates thoughts that are emitted from you like a beacon of light that shines for miles in all directions. Your messages will be received by like-minded recipients, and the Universe will set in motion the process to make your dreams become reality.

Change your surroundings

A very effective way of invoking a change in your emotional make-up is to change your environment. Take a trip, go on vacation, re-visit a place you have been to that has felt comforting, that brings back good memories.

Sometimes that place is deep within yourself, a memory of a time and place when you felt truly loved, safe and nurtured, although I would not recommend it for this exercise. Now you want to play, celebrate our newfound freedom, and plan for a new and exciting life!

And finally, seek out a skilled therapist

Therapy is always available and should be sought out in cases of extremely difficult experiences. A trained professional therapist can provide an environment of trust, a safe place where to discuss traumatic experiences, feelings of guilt, relationship issues and episodes of deep depression.

In fact, therapy is recommended in serious cases of

➢ Emotional distress

➢ Relationship issues

➢ Problems associated with coping mechanism

➢ Loss of a loved one

➢ Trauma and abuse

➢ Sexual problems and

➢ Clinical conditions

No one can tell you whether you need to see a therapist or not – you alone have to make that decision. Therapy has outgrown its role to fix the psyche; now it plays a role in personal growth and understanding of the self.

Recognition of the fact that therapy is needed is always the first step towards improvement.

〜

The thing always happens that you really believe in;
and the belief in a thing makes it happen.

Frank Loyd Wright

〜

Chapter 6

How To Reprint Your Blueprint For A Better And More Fulfilling Life

The really wonderful thing about the whole process of understanding and reprogramming the subconscious mind is that you don't have to wait until the health, wealth and wisdom arrive to enjoy the good feelings these things will bring to your life. By practicing the principles needed to reprogram your mind for success, you will already be experiencing all of the good emotions that having success will bring into your life.

You can feel the satisfaction of accomplishing great things, experience the feeling of glowing good health and enjoy the warm tingling feelings of being in love before the actual manifestation of these things happens in your life. Not only will you be moving yourself closer to success by doing these exercises to reprogram your subconscious mind, but you will already begin to experience the rewards of being successful in every area of your life.

Even if it takes you ten years to achieve all of the goals and desires you have for your life, it won't matter because your life will be better from the very moment you begin to understand and harness the power of your subconscious mind.

As you have learned in the previous chapters, you alone have created your blueprint and thus you alone have the power to change it. You have arrived at the crossroads of your destiny. You understand that you can change your life simply by changing your blueprint. You know that you are 100% responsible for your life and that everything others have told you since childhood about who you are and what your life's expectations are, have no more hold on you. You are not a victim anymore. You have escaped from the prison of your former thoughts and beliefs – you are FREE to start thinking right.

Follow the suggestions below and you will be sure to reprogram your subconscious mind and create a new blueprint for yourself that will lead you to a better and more fulfilled life!

Realize that you are not the same person today that you were yesterday, both physically and emotionally

Advances in scientific discoveries brought new understanding about the human body and confirmed that the building blocks of our body – the cells – regenerate themselves constantly. They grow, divide, and grow again and repeat this cycle over and over. In fact, no matter how old you are today, most of the cells in your body

are only 11 months old. The cells making up your bones regenerate too, only they can take up to seven years to complete the cycle. We are constantly changing.

So, you might ask – how come that the broken bone I had decades ago still shows up on an x-ray? And how come I look the same, just older with the passing years? Well, that's because of DNA and cell memory – what's impregnated in each individual cell gets passed on to its successor; out of the ashes of the Phoenix the newborn emerges.

Although we cannot change our genetic makeup, we can influence the deterioration of the body by making changes in what we eat, drink and how much we exercise, etc. For example, we know that stopping to smoke reverses a black lung and that stopping to drink alcohol excessively reverses the effects of cirrhosis of the liver, etc.

And so it is with the mind. While not a physical body, the mind is constantly changing too. The thoughts you have had since you were born have been imprinted in your subconscious together with all the experiences of a lifetime and emotions ever felt. These impressions influence your actions. You draw upon them to formulate your thoughts. And by the same process you perpetuate what's there, whether positive or negative – unless you consciously take action to change whatever is bothering you.

The scars generated by the negative blueprint that crippled you emotionally are still there today, and influence your thoughts and actions and have a tremendous effect on your happiness.

Listen to your inner voices

I met a young man once in India who taught me a valuable lesson. He was the driver assigned to me by an industrial company to take me to their various factories in the country. We spent a lot of time together in the car, passing time with idle chatter that soon led to discussions about his life and his family. Vasu was poorer than the poorest, at least by my standards, yet he carried himself like a man of great wealth, who had not a worry in the world.

I pried to get more information and quite accidentally he divulged his secret: his name, Vasu, means "wealth" in Sanskrit. Vasu's Inner Voices were telling him that he was blessed with wealth, and hence he was not bothered by the holes in his shoes. He saw abundance in what little he had, and did not focus on what he lacked. He was a very wise young man...

The image that you have of yourself is what shapes your destiny. Nothing else matters. For decades I had an image of myself that

held me back from achieving personal and professional fulfillment in spite of significant successes in business. My Inner Voices
(greatly influenced by my blueprint) were telling me that I could
never achieve great things – and I believed them. I second-guessed
myself every step of the way. The reversal of my fortunes came
when I started to change the way I thought about myself.

How do you judge yourself? Have you ever asked yourself "Why
did I do that?" or "What was I thinking?" Have you ever internally
chastised yourself for "being so stupid", for "acting like an idiot"?
Such words serve no purpose – they only tear you down, make you
feel unworthy and destroy your self esteem.

Think positive words. Train yourself to reject every negative
thought that comes into your mind. Never, ever voice a negative
thought about yourself, not even in jest! Every time you say something – positive or negative – it reinforces your belief in whatever
you expressed: if you say "I'll never get rid of those extra 10 lbs" –
guess what, you won't, until you train your Inner Voice to say: "I'm
fabulous, and those extra 10 lbs will come off in a jiffy!"

Build your self-esteem. Your personal transformation begins when
you can identify and deal with your shortcomings. Even though
you are changing your outlook on life to a more positive view, remember that no one is perfect. Perfection is a state of mind that
everyone strives for, but you should always learn to be happy with
what you can do. It is not healthy to become distraught over what
you cannot do. Make your goals reachable in order to be successful. Use the power of positive thinking and the ability of positive
words to change your destiny.

Start challenging your inner voices now. Start thinking right!

Thinking right begins with the question: What do you want out
of life? Are you living your passion? Do you know what your passion is? Are you satisfied with your life, with the choices you made
along the way that got you where you are today? Did you really

How about just living your life instead of living up to the expectations of others? go to college because you wanted to and studied what you pleased, or were there other forces that influenced you?

Are you in a job that is challenging, that you love, or would you rather be doing something else? Are you secretly yearning to be a saxophone player at a nightclub, but will not admit to it because...? What is the reason that is holding you back? Would working with horses and other animals on a farm be more appealing than battling rush hour every day of the week? How about just living your life instead of living up to the expectations of others?

Know what you really want out of life

One of the main reasons why many people do not get what they want in life is that they are not sure of what they want! You will find many people who express, either occasionally or on a regular basis, that they are unhappy, unfulfilled, and dissatisfied with themselves or their lives. They know that there is something they want from life, something which would lead them to feel better, happier, and more fulfilled – but they do not know what it is!

If this sounds like you, you will be glad to know that your life can change for the better! One of the most important keys in finding or acquiring what one wants in life is to know, with clear certainty, exactly what it is. Whether you want a new car, a better job, a happier marriage, a stronger sense of purpose, or any number of other possibilities, putting your deepest desires into words is the first step toward reaching what you want the most.

After you have acknowledged your wishes, you can then begin to remove the obstacles which stand in the way of attaining them, as well as build on the strengths and assets which you already have in your favor. You will be giving yourself the best possible chance of realizing your wishes and reaching your goals when you have a clear sense of who you are and what you have to contribute to bringing them into reality.

Not knowing what you really want out of your life can have long lasting consequences in terms of years wasted, low personal and job satisfaction and your overall state of unhappiness. I know, because I speak from experience. Let me share with you how I managed to make a misguided decision during my career at the World Bank – because I listened to my blueprint instead of my heart:

Alone in the Board Room

The top echelon of the World Bank, all 200 plus Vice Presidents and Directors, are gathered together in the Board room. Three rows of extra chairs have been brought in to accommodate everyone. I am seated next to one of the Vice Presidents, who points at a familiar face here and there and tells me bits and pieces of gossip – always a favorite pastime among WB staff, no matter what level they hold. Soon the chatter in the room dies down as the President of the Bank enters and makes his way to the head of the conference table. He takes a quick look around, sits down and begins his address: "Gentlemen" he says, "the purpose of this meeting is to ……"

As I dutifully sit at full attention, eyes and ears on the speaker, I feel a sharp jab in my ribs. "Stand up" says the VP next to me, "Stand up, so he can see you!" and with another jab he practically pushes me off the chair – so I stand up. At first the droning voice of the President continues without interruption, but soon there is rustling and whispering as heads turn in my direction; the voices get louder and now everyone is looking at me – I freeze in total embarrassment and don't know what to do. Now even the President has spied me – the lone woman at the other end of the table, lost among a sea of men.

There is a moment of total, unbearable silence – and then he claps his hands together and begins anew: "Lady and Gentlemen…." Roaring applause from 200 men drowns out the rest of the sentence. Blood is rushing to my cheeks, a trickle of sweat runs down my back – still, I keep my composure, nod slightly in each direction, and then glide back onto my seat, glad to be invisible again as the attention once more returns to the President and his important address.

I never liked being the center of attention. As a child I used to climb under the table when asked to recite a kindergarten poem or sing a song. Being invisible meant being safe. Alas, it was impossible to be invisible as the only woman Director at the World Bank. I was in a glass house with every one of my actions or non-actions being visible to the rest of the world and I was very uncomfortable playing this role.

I had joined the World Bank at the Manager level just four years earlier. I loved my job, particularly the traveling. In the better part of a decade that I spent with the Bank I traveled the world several times over. I have been to 98 countries in my life and have actually seen a good part of each one of them.

Seeing the world and learning to understand different cultures and traditions has been an incredible experience for me. I have seen both the opulent and the impoverished. I have been guest in a Sheik's Bedouin tent at the foot of the  Atlas Mountains in Morocco that was furnished with greater luxuries than you can find in the richest palaces of the world. And I have been a guest in a Masai hut in Kenya, where ten people and their livestock live in a space no larger than 15'x15' and only five feet high. I met with presidents of countries and broke bread with the poorest of the poor. I slept in the luxurious private guest houses of the rich, as well as on military cots under heavy mosquito netting when visiting remote areas in Africa. It did not matter to me. I felt alive and on top of the world.

My glorious field work was abruptly cut short when I accepted the promotion to Director. I transitioned from total freedom of travel, setting my own schedule, working entirely on my own with a small staff to practically no travel, being prisoner to schedules set by others, running a 30 plus employee department, to becoming a role model and being in the glass house – all within a short period of time.

My life changed drastically. Instead of feeling confident and proud, knowing that someone in some part of the world was glad I shared my knowledge and experience with them, I felt insecure having to defend my every word and action in front of other leaders in the Boardroom. Instead of showing a clerk at a tea plantation in Uganda how to record invoices in his ledgers, I was sorting out staff issues in Washington. Instead of assisting a production manager in a fish hatchery in Thailand to prepare inventory records, I was writing endless interoffice memoranda or rewriting reports drafted by others.

I felt caged in. I did not want to be a role model for all the women at the Bank. I had no tolerance for petty arguments and I did not want to be a referee in disputes. I felt I was wasting my time climbing up the corporate ladder I had really no aspirations to ascend.

Reflecting back on these years "in the Boardroom" as I like to call them, I often wondered why I took a path that suited me so little. How could I have misjudged the work I would be doing at headquarters as compared to in the field? Why did I not see the pitfalls that would make me unhappy and unfulfilled in my job?

I could not see it then, but I can see it now. Yes, you guessed it – I was following my blueprint, the blueprint that dictated my behavior and my actions – to be stronger, better and more powerful than all others so I would be safe. Being a Director of the World Bank signaled to others that I was a person to be reckoned with, someone of stature, someone with power. Job satisfaction was irrelevant for as long as the blueprint was satisfied....

Do not make the same mistakes I made! Identify your talents, find your passion and rethink your values! Make sure these are your own and not those of your spouse, or members of your family or friends. This is of course easier said than done, because the things you do on a daily basis might be so ingrained in your soul that you might actually believe that they are your passion!

It's time to go back to the drawing board.

Find your passion in life

Some people know early on what they want out of life and they build their lives around their passion and generally live a happy and fulfilled life. But if you are like most people, you probably can't remember your passion or even if you ever had one. You go through life like a robot, getting up every day, going to work - to a job you took on because it pays you money, not because you love it - and you spend your idle time watching movies or television and daydream about the life you could have had.

When you have passion, you love every moment of your life. You have purpose and that gets your juices flowing and brings on your creativity, your vision and inspiration to do great things. There is spring in your step as you strive resolutely to accomplish the tasks you have set for yourself every day. Time flies and you enjoy every success, no matter how big or small. You feel like reaching for the sky.

Finding your passion again is not that difficult. You just have to ask yourself a few questions and concentrate on your answers. Assume for this exercise that neither money nor time nor any limitations exist that would get in the way of your perfect life. Listen to your heart when you answer these questions:

➤ What do I really love to do?

➤ Where would I love to live?

➤ How would I love to live?

➤ With whom would I love to live?

➤ What would my ideal day, month, year be like?

➤ What would I spend my money on?

➤ What activities would I engage in?

➤ What would my perfect lifestyle be?

Write down any and all answers that come to your mind, even if they are in conflict of each other at the moment. Do not think of your current life, think only of your dreams, your ambitions and your desires. Think back to your childhood and remember what you loved to do then; then examine whether these interests still exist now, or whether they have faded with the years and ascension into adulthood.

Make a list of at least three answers for each question and then walk away from your list for a day or two. When you next look at what you have written down, start evaluating and prioritizing your answers. When you do this you will soon see a thread running through these answers that link you with your true passion.

For example, you might find that you have listed an outdoor activity or life style for each of the above questions, such as: I'd really love to sail around the world; I'd love to live by the ocean in a casual setting with lots of good friends; I'd go fishing every day or hang out with the local folks and help them with their work; my money would go to fixing up the pier and paying for repair work on some of the fishermen's boats; I would play tennis, swim a lot, do some parasailing and perhaps deep sea diving; my life would be simple and totally satisfying.

If you describe this as your perfect life – your passion is not to go fishing and play tennis, although these are preferred activities – your true passion is to help other people, as this is what makes you happy. And when you know what makes you happy, then you'll be able to find ways to be happy without having to sail around the world to capture the feeling of happiness.

Rethink your values

From the following list of values, presented in no particular order, select ten that best represent what you need to experience in your life in order to be happy. Feel free to add other values to this list:

➢ Results – must achieve results

➢ Self Direction – must have autonomy in my life

➢ Beauty – must have beauty and beautiful things in my life

➢ Harmony – must have harmony and be harmonious with others

➢ Freedom – must be free to express myself

➢ Adventure – must have excitement in my life

➢ Duty and responsibility – must meet all of my obligations

➢ Learning – love to discover things and learn

➢ Security – must feel secure in my profession, job, family and life

➢ Integrity – must be truthful in all respects

➢ Power – must be in charge, must have power to get things done

➢ Spirituality – must be connected to my higher power

➢ Loyalty – must be loyal and receive loyalty from others

➢ Excellence – must master my profession and deliver excellence

➢ Serenity – must be calm and clear in my mind

➢ Orderliness – must have structure and organization in my life

➢ Nature – love nature and must be connected with it

➤ Fun – must have play time and pleasure in my life

➤ Giving – must do good works and give to others

➤ Vision – must be creative and have creativity in my life

➤ Humor – must laugh often to be happy

➤ Recognition – must be appreciated for my actions

➤ Justice – must have justice and honor in my life

➤ Wisdom – must have knowledge

When you have compiled your list of ten values, put them in order of priority, and then evaluate on a scale of one to ten, how you currently measure up to them. For example, if you value Integrity the highest on your list of values, measure your achievement against it. If you are honest and truthful to yourself in this evaluation, and find that you score only a six, you will know where to place emphasis in the future.

Your talents, passion and values will become the foundation for your new blueprint. You are going to re-program your subconscious mind with new instructions – and these instructions better be based on your real values, beliefs and opinions!

The point is this – look at your life and be honest with yourself. Don't waste any more time. Don't make decisions based on someone else's values. Know your own values and act on them. Spend some time to reflect on the dreams you had when you were young and then ask yourself what it would take to make them come true today.

Develop your talents

If you are like most people you have one or several talents that you can express your creativity with and become successful at. It is important to explore all of your talents and take the time to develop and perfect them as much as possible. If Rembrandt had spent all of his time working in a factory and then sat in his rocking chair for hours each day after work contemplating his navel, we would have never heard of him nor seen his amazing works of art. Don't cheat yourself or the world by wasting your life away on unimportant things. Take the time to develop your creativity and see where it leads you. Your passion and talents might interrelate – or they might not, it does not matter. What matters is your determination and resolution to make the best of your talents and to use them to further your objective of creating your perfect, blissful and totally fulfilled life.

Do not live by the opinions of others

Back home in Austria "what would the neighbors say!" was our mother's standard reply when we children wanted something out of the ordinary. Come home after dark – out of the question, what would the neighbors say? Wear the latest fashion to school – no way, what would the neighbors say! Get bad grades, or get in trouble – what will the neighbors say?

We lived by the opinions of our neighbors, and so we learned to value the opinions of others before we thought about our own wishes and desires. In my case, deferring to others, letting them dictate my life was reinforcing the other side of my blueprint – I am worthless, I can't make a difference. Better to hide, to be invisible, let others have opinions...

Use hypnosis and meditation to re-program your subconscious mind

As discussed earlier, another tool that, when used properly, has been proven to be effective in reprogramming the subconscious mind is hypnosis. By achieving an altered state of consciousness, during hypnosis contact is made directly with the subconscious mind and positive suggestions are inserted directly into the subconscious.

Whatever method is used, it is important that you believe in the process and that the right positive messages are used. It is also important that you continue to reinforce the positive messages

The positive thoughts in your subconscious will not grow without proper care

with your actions so that you become deeply rooted in the subconscious. Just like planting seeds, if they are only tossed on the surface and not watered the seeds will not grow. The positive thoughts in your subconscious will not grow without proper care either.

Meditation is also a valuable tool for communicating with and changing the programming of the subconscious mind. You can meditate on the actual goals you are trying to accomplish or you can meditate on positive attributes you are trying to develop in yourself. As noted above, the main goal with meditation is to block out all other thoughts and external stimuli so that your thoughts become very focused which increases their strength and power.

Stay in the present

You want to do everything in your power to create the feelings and emotions of having the success and freedom you desire right now. By placing a future date on your desire, you are giving your mind permission to wait until that date to take action and make changes.

When your mind waits until the date you have chosen to begin to change, your conscious mind will see that the goal has not been reached by the designated date and interpret that as a failure. This in turn will program your subconscious mind with negative thoughts and emotions again and put a hindrance on your forward progress.

And finally, complete this Exercise:

Reprint your blueprint and achieve anything you want in life!

Re-programming your subconscious mind to achieve greater health, wealth and happiness is possible for you now that you know how the subconscious mind works. It is simply a matter of using your five senses: touch, taste, smell, sound and sight and then having the right internal dialogue (positive) to evoke the emotion you want to associate with that aspect of your life.

This can be used in any area of your life to achieve virtually anything you want to achieve. Successful people have used this information to achieve everything from curing their own cancer to finding the spouse of their dreams to making millions of dollars.

There is nothing in the universe that is out of your reach once you truly understand how to reprogram your subconscious mind. You will be able to achieve absolutely anything that you can imagine, if you believe in it and take action.

> *There is nothing in the universe that is out of your reach once you truly understand how to reprogram your subconscious...*

This is not folklore or magic, it is scientific fact. Even though the medical community can't give us all the answers as to the exact physical explanation of how this works, every study that is done gives new relevance to the power of the subconscious mind.

You must know exactly what you want to achieve in each area of your life including your health and fitness goals, financial goals, spiritual goals and educational goals. But let these goals be yours – not someone else's!

Now it is time to put your new blueprint down on paper and make it yours to live by from now on. Ask yourself the same questions we explored in Chapter 4 and write your answers to them in the table on the next page.

Then think about how you feel now about your life and your future, in light of what you now know about your old blueprint, how it was formed, how it no longer serves you, and how you have grown in your understanding of your subconscious mind and your ability to influence it. Think about your values today, your passions and your talents and what you really want out of life.

How do you feel about	Old Blueprint	New Blueprint
Yourself		
People		
The World		
Your Future		

Here is an example of how this table might look like once completed:

How do you feel about	Old Blueprint	New Blueprint
Yourself	Incompetent, unloved, insecure, afraid, lonely	Competent, confident, brave, loved
People	Untrustworthy, cruel, unkind, malicious, hurtful, deceiving	Honest, kind, caring, considerate, compassionate,
The world	Bad place to live, uninviting, desolate, depressing, cold, harsh	Great place to live and raise a family, welcoming, hospitable, warm and wonderful
Your future	Bleak, miserable, hopeless	Fabulous, secure, happy, bright

Now write your New Blueprint, substituting your words for my example words (see next page):

My New Blueprint

I am competent

I am confident

I am brave

I am loved

People are honest

People are kind and reliable

People are caring

People are considerate

People are compassionate

The world is a great place to live and raise a family

The world is welcoming

The world is hospitable

The world is warm and wonderful

My future is fabulous

My future is secure

My future is happy

My future is bright

Look for the signs of success

As you start to implement your new blueprint in your life, look for the signs of success. Be open to the promptings and opportunities that become available to you now. You will begin to receive inspirations and find yourself "in the right place at the right time".

Expect this, look for it and be prepared to act on the inspiration and information you are given. New ideas of things to do and say will pop into your mind when you least expect it. Don't ignore these even if they seem a little "out there". In order to start having and achieving things you have never had before, you have to do things differently than you have ever done before.

Jim D. of Roanoke, VA told me this intriguing story:

I was driving down highway 81 one Friday night on my way home to visit my Mom, when something possessed me to make a stop at this rest station. I had enough gas to get where I was going, and I had not planned on stopping for food, so I don't know why I stopped. I went into the Diner, which was pretty full as would be the case on a Friday night when everyone is on the road for the weekend. The only free seat I could find was at the counter, so I steered myself there and sat down between two big guys who looked like truck drivers. I ordered a cup of coffee and picked up the local newspaper that had been left on my seat by someone.

As I opened the paper, I almost fell off my chair – staring at me was the picture of an old school friend of mine, who, according to the caption under the photograph, was now the Mayor of the little town where I had stopped. I read on and learned that a regional shopping mall construction project was underway there and that the contractor had defaulted on the contract.

I was getting excited at that point, because I am a contractor myself and I'd been looking for a change in my life at that point. I'd been into residential construction and wanted to move into commercial, but did not know how, since I did not know anyone who would consider me, inexperienced as I was in this side of the business. I decided right then and there that I would stay overnight and find my Mayor friend in the morning to see if he would take a chance with me...

To make a long story short, I built a great shopping mall and had a very successful career in commercial real estate after that. None of this would have happened, had I not followed my hunch...

Having written your new blueprint is a great start, but it is not all you need to do to change your life to a better one. Now you have to put new structures in place that will keep you anchored and help you achieve your goals.

The best way to prepare for life is to begin to live.

Elbert Hubbard

Chapter 7

Create New Structures In Your Life

Let's take a look at this perfect life, this dream life you've always wanted. What are the elements that promise to bring eternal happiness to everyone who can achieve it? Is this life really different for each one of us or are we all searching for the same thing, like the same gift just wrapped up in a different package?

Why do you need new structures in your life?

Like a high rise building or a bridge that spans the oceans, without the foundation and the structures that are anchored to it, they would be unstable and could collapse at any time. As you know from Chapter 1, in the construction industry we use steel and concrete and the strongest materials known to man to manufacture these structures. We take no chances and often design and build for structural loads that far exceed the anticipated ones.

Why would you do things differently when building your new life? You want to have the strongest foundation and structures in place that you can imagine. You need support in every aspect of your life, so you will never fail again. These structures are created through other people who support your values and passions, and your relationships with them.

You also need to make changes in the way you behave, how you think about yourself and how you feel about yourself and others. Implement the following suggestions and see how quickly you will become anchored in your new blueprint that will carry you to great heights, achievements and happiness!

Surround yourself with people you trust

Take a good look at your friends and associates. I know you love them, they've been at your side since childhood perhaps and you've shared lots of memorable – and not so memorable experiences. Here is Bob, your high school buddy, who laughs at all your bad jokes, or Helen, your cheer leader/sorority friend, who adores you and can always be counted on to accompany you on a shopping spree at the local mall.

These friends are great – but are they really the kind of people you could rely on for emotional support and guidance towards a better and more fulfilled life? Where are Bob and Helen now in their own journey of life? Are they happy and fulfilled? Are they living the life they want and always have dreamt about? How do they react when you tell them about your dreams? Do they support your ideas or do they put you down, telling you to forget about them, that you are full of nonsense, that you should stick to what you know, to stop being a dreamer?

If this describes your friends' attitudes and advice to you, they are not the kind of people you need now. You should surround yourself with new friends who can indeed help you achieve your dreams.

To find such new friends look around you in all areas of your life – your job, your church, your golf or athletic club perhaps, and this time take notice of the leaders. Who's the boss, who's on the Board of Directors, who's making the decisions, who's well liked and trusted? What are others saying about them? What are the qualities that make them stand out of the crowds? Study their faces – do you see kindness and empathy in them?

Look at the face of Nelson Mandela. If you never heard his name and had no idea of his background, what would you read from his face? Aside from good looks, there is the ever present smile, the twinkle in his eyes. Absent are frown lines and puck-ered brows. This is the face of a man who spent two decades incarcerated as a political prisoner, yet there is no bitterness, no anger, no resentment visible in it. I read gentleness, compassion, benevolence, kindheartedness and sympathy in this face and would trust this man instantly.

If you like what you see in the faces of new acquaintances, stick around, learn as much as you can about them, become their apprentice if possible and emulate what they do, model your approach to everything on how they approach it. If, on the other hand, you do not like what you see in these people, walk away and keep looking until you find your mentor or life coach.

You need both supporters and mentors in your life. A supporter is someone who believes in you, someone who understands the journey you have embarked on to change your life for the better, someone who will encourage you, help you along the way, be there for you when you need emotional support or a shoulder to cry on when the road ahead seems rough at times.

A mentor on the other hand, is a teacher, a person helping another one to achieve something important in life. In mentoring, the mentor and mentee establish an informal relationship in which to discuss issues, standards, integrity, loyalty and a host of professional or personal topics, whatever the mentee is interested in exploring.

It helps if the mentor is experienced in the relevant subject matter, but that is not always necessary. For example, your grandfather could be your mentor, simply by supporting you in your quest to become a better person. By being there for you, listening to you and encouraging you to share your most personal thoughts and desires, he could have a greater influence on your life than all your other teachers combined. Confidentiality is of course paramount to an effective mentoring relationship.

Seek out people who are the kind of person you want to be

Change the type of people you associate with. If you want to over-come drug addiction, you need to only associate with people who live a successful, drug-free lifestyle. If you want to be wealthy, you need to associate with wealthy people. If you want to be thinner, you need to hang out with thinner people. This is not to say that you don't care for the other people who are a part of your life or that you should start to discriminate against anybody, but keep in mind that you are not only judged by the company you keep, you also have a tendency to be like them.

The more you spend time with people who are the type of people you want to become, the more you will be like them. Remember what you have learned about how the subconscious mind is pro-grammed and this will instantly make sense to you. The experiences and emotions you have while spending time with healthy, wealthy, wise and happy people will program your subconscious mind with the thoughts and ideas that will help you become healthy, wealthy, wise and happy too.

Be grateful for what you already have

You may have heard the saying that there are two times when it is absolutely essential to be grateful: when your life is good, and when it is horrible! This is precisely the reason why being grateful is so important – because it puts you in the position of not taking anything for granted!

You might think it is very easy to be grateful when everything in your life seems fine, when everything is going along the way you want it to, and your daily life is basically stress-free and without any serious problems or complications. If you put some thought into it, though, how often is this actually the case? Even when life seems "almost perfect," don't you still wish for that little extra bit which would make it one-hundred-percent perfect?

This is how you learn to be grateful! While it is only human nature to wish for something more, instead of crying for what you don't have try being grateful for everything you do have! Whichever specific aspects of your life you focus on the most, you will soon appreciate it much more when you get the hang of being grateful. Appreciating your life is the surest way to enjoy it to its fullest!

...instead of crying for what you don't have try being grateful for everything you do have!

The idea of being grateful when your life is filled with negativity may seem strange at first, even impossible. However, if you put some careful thought into the things for which you can be grateful for, you will begin to shift your focus from the negative factors in your life to the positive factors. Your outlook itself will start to shift, becoming less negative and more positive.

Even in the worst of times there is something for which you can be grateful. Making a "Gratitude List" not only creates the best atmosphere for this but also gives you your own words to look back on when old uncertainties try to take over. Whichever method you feel will work the best for you, it can benefit you in ways you haven't even dreamed were possible!

What are you grateful for in your life? What inspires you to be thankful? When you begin by pondering, you will probably come up with many more factors than you had initially thought existed.

Whether your life is currently quite good, or whether it is medio-cre, or whether your daily life is overflowing with difficulties, when you put some time into considering what you are truly grateful for – your outlook will begin to transform!

Be free of self-doubt forever

If you suffer from self-doubt, you probably know that it can affect nearly every aspect of your life. Self-doubt can affect your performance on the job, how effective you are at setting goals and making plans, and your interactions with other people.

Self doubt has its roots in the negative messages you were told as a child. After all, everything that a child "knows" about himself is what he was told – and he carries these messages with him throughout his life. If those messages were negative, you continue to feel their impact, and you continue to base how and what you think about yourself on those messages. You may believe that you are not intelligent, that you are not adequate, that you basically "do not have what it takes" – all because these are the messages you received when you were young, and which are now embedded in your blueprint!

Self doubt has its roots in the negative messages you were told as a child.

As you know now, you can re-write your old blueprint. You can go back to those old negative messages – and you can replace them with positive, more appropriate messages which will benefit you today and in the future. In other words, you can look at the things you were told about yourself which were not correct, and replace them with self-affirming messages that are true!

For example, your parent or your teacher may have told you were not smart. Perhaps the person was just having a bad day, or perhaps he or she was the type of person who liked to treat people in a negative manner. Whichever the case was, you can now inform yourself that what the person said was not true – it did not reflect your intelligence, your abilities.

When you begin defining yourself with self-affirming, factual messages, you will see that the things told to you in the past will lose their power. Old messages will no longer have a serious impact on your life – and you can be free of self-doubt forever!

Love yourself – it's more important than you think!

You have probably heard the old saying "In order to love anyone else, you must love yourself first." If you are like most of us, you have probably heard it many times over the years, yet never really figured out what it meant or why it was relevant. The fact is that if you do not think well of yourself, it shows – it influences the way you interact with other people, the way you treat yourself, and even your basic outlook.

Holding yourself in high regard is important; but perhaps an even better way of looking at self-love is by using the term self-acceptance. When you view it from this perspective, you will probably be able to easily see that it does not exist in degrees: you either do, or you do not.

If you have not developed a healthy sense of self-love it's probably so because you were taught the exact opposite.

You may wonder why it is so difficult to look at yourself and accept yourself. If you have not developed a healthy sense of self-love it's probably so because you were taught the exact opposite. While many people were "taught" to not love or accept themselves all the way back in the early childhoods, many others have experienced this type of negativity in their adult lives. Women, especially, often become victimized by partners whose abusive tactics include diminishing the women's sense of self-acceptance and self-love.

Now is the time for you to begin to acknowledge yourself as a worthwhile human being – a person who has true value in simply being yourself.

The lack of self-love often comes from lowering your expectations of yourself to meet the negative messages of other people. You can begin to break the hold that this has had on you by empowering yourself with positive affirmations. Letting go of other people's negative definitions of who you are and what you are all about is a good start; but the fundamental aspect of learning how to love and accept yourself goes much further than that.

Regardless of how much potential you may have, how much talent, how much ability, while these factors are important, they do not sum up who you really are. It is only when you have begun to see yourself as a person of worth and value, from nothing more nor less than being yourself, that you will start to experience self-love and self-acceptance. When you can do this, you will be amazed at the impact it has on you, and the impact it will have on your life!

Have a positive attitude – it will make a world of difference!

You probably know someone who has a negative attitude and often displays it. If so, you are already familiar with the complications which usually result from this – people do not like to be around him, and it can even interfere with his job. It can affect one's work obligations, social life, and basic interpersonal relating.

What if you are a person like this? What if you have a negative out-look, and it is spilling over into various aspects of your life? Even if your job performance has been suffering, or if people are no longer welcoming your company, you do not need to live with these consequences – because you do not need to hold onto the attitude which has caused them!

A positive attitude can make a world of difference! Soon after you have begun to apply this principle, you will see this for yourself!

Negativity will only hold you down; a positive attitude will help bring you back up. Negativity will keep you focused on everything that is wrong, everything that has ever been wrong; but a positive attitude will bring your focus to everything that is right and better. The very best way to look at the subject, though, is to remind yourself that while a negative attitude will limit you, a positive attitude will go a long way in getting rid of those limits. If you think about how much a negative attitude has limited you, this in itself should be a great motivating factor!

Negativity will only hold you down; a positive attitude will help bring you back up.

Most people do not like to acknowledge that they are limiting themselves and their prospects with their own attitudes and behavior. When you start to replace the "cannot" with "can," you will see how much power there is in your own attitude! You will feel that you have more potential, as well as the ability to reach your potential – while the only thing that has actually changed is your own attitude! Goal-setting and making plans will become much easier, and you will find that you can accomplish much more than you had previously thought you could!

When you take on a new, positive attitude, you will experience wonderful results with other people. Instead of shying away from a chronic complainer who rarely had anything uplifting to say, people will appreciate your company when your positive attitude makes itself apparent in your personal interactions.

A positive attitude will work wonders in how you feel about yourself, also. Instead of always looking for what's wrong in yourself and in your life, you will gain a newfound appreciation for everything that is good in both. You will find that you like your life more than you did before – and that you like yourself better, too!

If you are not yet convinced, perhaps you would like to give it a try! Whenever you sense one of those old negative thoughts, feelings, or ideas preparing to creep in, let them go and replace them with something good, upbeat, and positive. It will not be long before you experience results!

Use your creativity to find satisfaction in life

So many people live their lives as though it is something that just "happens" to them. This is very sad because they are unaware that they are creating their own life and so they live their lives by default usually ending up with disappointment, depression and fear. Every single person on earth has the power to create his own life. Using that power brings us the greatest satisfaction and happiness that life has to offer. One of the ways we create our own lives is to use our creativity.

There are countless ways you can express your creativity and each one of them brings intense satisfaction...

Our creativity can be expressed in many different ways. Some people express their creativity by writing stories or poetry. Others express it with artistic expressions ranging from painting or drawing to sculpting to sewing or other types of crafts. Still other people express their creativity through interior design, make-up artistry or hairdressing. There are countless ways you can express your creativity and each one of them brings intense satisfaction, happiness and fulfillment to you if you allow yourself to fully use the capacity for creativity that exists within you.

Find your motivation in life

What is motivation? The dictionary describes it as "the act of giving somebody a reason or incentive to do something" or "a feeling of enthusiasm, interest or commitment that makes somebody want to do something". So, motivation can be the reason you do something or the feeling that makes you want to do something.

Finding your motivation in life is about finding a reason to succeed and about creating and nurturing the feelings that make you want to be successful. When a person has gone through a tragedy, such as losing a loved one, sometimes they struggle with finding the motivation to get out of bed in the morning.

Once you have found your true motivation there will be no circumstance that can stop you from wanting to get out of bed, in fact, the things that might be considered tragedies or setbacks to someone else will only make you try harder to succeed.

Think about two runners competing in a race for a moment. Both of them are about the same height, weight and have about the same degree of muscle tone. Each of them has trained equally hard and pushed his physical body to the limit during practices and compe-  titions throughout the year. Now imagine for a moment that one of these runners has just lost a loved one. It was his grandmother who had raised him since his mother left when he was just two years old. His grandmother always told him to do his very best.

The runners take their marks and this runner pictures his grand-mother cheering him on. He wants to win this race to honor her memory. Which runner do you think will win the race? The runner with the greatest motivation will surely win, every time. It would not matter if he had a pulled muscle, headache or any other challenge that day. His motivation is so great that it will overcome anything that stands in his way.

Each and every person has something or someone that motivates them. Some people find their motivation in wanting to make the most of the gifts they feel they were endowed with by their creator. Other people find it in the love of their children. For some it is their own sense of contentment and satisfaction. Some people are motivated by money or power and others by feelings of love and commitment.

Every person is unique in his talents and abilities, as well as his motivation to use his gifts successfully.

A person who is not doing anything with her life or at least not achieving any level of success may think that she just doesn't have any motivation, but this is usually not true. Sometimes it just takes a little work to uncover it. Many people do waste their lives away and never know their purpose or their motivation, but this does not have to be your choice.

Within you lies the ability to succeed and find satisfaction, fulfillment and purpose in your life. Taking the time to think about and uncover your hidden motivation can be the difference between a life of purpose and happiness and one of just survival. Your success begins the moment you make the decision to go after it.

Respect yourself and others

Respect can refer to feelings of esteem, admiration, consideration and thoughtfulness. Notice that none of these words are based on fear or control. You can't force someone to respect you no matter how hard you try (in fact attempts at this usually backfire and create feelings of resentment) and you can't force yourself to respect someone else. You can make yourself act respectfully towards someone, but that doesn't mean you respect them. If you truly want others to respect you or have the ability to respect others, you have to respect yourself first. Having a healthy self esteem is the first step in having healthy relationships with others and healthy relationships with others are vital to a successful life.

Respect yourself first

So, how do you learn to respect yourself? The first step is to treat yourself with respect. Even before the feelings are there you can begin with the positive behaviors that exude respect. Don't berate yourself no matter how bad you "mess up", not even in your head. Thoughts are powerful and must be monitored vigilantly to maintain or create a healthy self-esteem and the type of positive attitude that will bring you success both in relationships and in material things.

Give yourself the benefit of the doubt. Focus on what you are doing well and then do more of that. Do things that benefit the lives of others. Serving others is a great way to feel better about yourself and begins a self-perpetuating cycle of good feelings. Small acts of kindness and thoughtfulness help build respect of yourself.

Treating other people with respect also helps you better respect yourself. Do you respect a person who is always negative or berating other people whether it is to their faces or behind their backs? You won't respect this type of behavior in yourself, either. Don't even think negative thoughts about anyone. Respect is created by positive behaviors and emotions. You feel much better about yourself when you recognize that everyone is human and we all make mistakes.

Forgiving yourself and others quickly and easily brings peace, happiness and contentment into your life and helps you have greater respect for yourself and everyone else. Focus on the positive and things get even more positive. Look for the best in everyone (including yourself) and you will be surprised how much good you can find.

Change your words

The power of positive words will change your destiny from a negative outlook to a positive one. You must believe in your positive words in order to achieve positive thinking. You are what you say!

Eliminate negative words from your vocabulary.

Negative word	Really means	Positive words
can't	don't know or don't want to	will do or can do
maybe	need more information	yes or no
I'll try to	attempt, struggle or test	I will
I think I'll be able to	contemplate, ponder	I know I will
but	negates what was stated before	and
if	condition	when
problem	hindrance, setback	challenge, situation, growth opportunity
have to	must	want to
hopefully, I hope to	I don't believe this will happen	I will
just kidding	not playing full out	say nothing instead

When your words are positive – that is what changes your destiny. Your attitude becomes positive with your words. Your success rate becomes positive with your words. Your spoken positive words are the keys to your transformation.

Create a vision board

A vision board acts like a magnet that attracts what you really want into your life. It also serves as visual reminder that keeps you and your mind (including your subconscious mind) on what you are going after. Your mind will automatically notice things that will bring you closer to your goals. Your mind will think and come up with ideas that will realize what is on your vision board.

To create an effective vision board, first you have to divide your life into several general categories. The common categories are like health, wealth, career, relationship, emotional and spiritual. Brainstorm a few categories that you want to focus on in your life. You should also balance your life because you want all parts of your life to be doing well!

The next thing you need to do is to decide whether you want to make a vision board for each category or you want to create a single vision board that combines all these categories. I would recommend that you do one for each category.

To create a vision board for a category, health for example, find pictures from magazines, newspapers and other media that have pictures which represent your ideal health and fitness. It can be pictures of an athlete, a model, a person exercising, or healthy foods. The most important thing is that the pictures should make you excited! If you had the body of perfect fitness and lived the life of perfect health just as in

the pictures, how would you feel? If the pictures do not excite you enough, look for more!

Another example might be the things that you want to have. If a picture of a race car does not excite you enough, maybe that is not what you really want. Try other pictures such as a jet plane or a helicopter! Let your mind go wild. Don't set any limitation to yourself! Be a child and let your heart and desires drive you.

Other than pictures, you can also use words. If you are doing a vision board on relationships, you can cut out words like "Passionate Relationship", "Ultimate Lover", "Sexy Moments", "Lover of My Life" or the like.

You want to combine pictures and words to give a deeper effect. If you are doing a vision board on health, cut out words like "Athlete", "Adonis", "Iron Man", "Perfect Health", "Strong and Powerful Body", "Role Model of Health" or "Holistic Health". Similar to pictures, these words should excite you. Read through the magazine or websites to get some ideas of phrases that really excite you. If you find it through your computer, print it out and put it on your vision board.

Combine all the pictures and words and paste them together to form a vision board. If you are creating only one vision board for all categories, make sure you have a balance and include pictures and words for each category. Again, you want to excel in all areas of your life.

Finally, look at it again and make sure it really motivates you and drives you to make it happen! Hang your vision board in a place that you will look at every single day.

You can now make the Law of Attraction work for you immediately by using creative visualization. You can create the life that you want by first creating the images in your head. This is because you will attract whatever you consistently visualize.

Why does visualization cause the attraction process to take place? Wallace D. Wattles in "The Science of Getting Rich", wrote that in order for you to attract anything into your life, you have to believe with conviction that you will receive what you asked for. One of the best ways to make your mind believe what you asked for will come true is by doing visualization.

When you believe that you can achieve something, you send out a stronger energy. You are more confident and you will perform better. People will pick up your level of energy on a subconscious level and will respond to you positively. This is true in business, relationships, health and especially in sports. Rebecca Smith, a clinical research assistant in sports psychology at the U.S. Olympic Training center in Colorado, said that professional athletes spend a good deal of time visualizing their victory by telling their minds exactly what they want their bodies to achieve.

> *When you believe that you can achieve something, you send out a stronger energy.*

Visualize consistently all the things or events you want in your life and they will show up for you. Believe this and see it happen!

Here are the experiences of two of my students who combined several of my suggestions and techniques:

Maria A. of Washington, DC says:

> *I really, really, really wanted to have a vacation apartment on the ocean; I dreamed about it every night and spent every free time in Ocean City, the closest beach resort to Washington. I knew all the stores along the famous boardwalk and had already made friends with lots of people that lived there. After taking your course, I decided to manifest my dream vacation apartment by visualizing living in it and starting a vision board. I took pictures of one particularly attractive apartment building in Ocean City and then asked the building manager whether there were any units available for rent or purchase. This got me a private showing of a two bed-*

room apartment for sale with a fabulous view of the ocean. I took pictures and put them up on my vision board, and never thought about the fact that I could not possibly afford such a wonderful and luxurious place.

Summer turned to winter and trips to the ocean were not practical. Still, I kept dreaming about "my vacation place on the beach" and focused my desire on it every day without fail. Come Spring, a surprise letter arrived from my cousin from Nova Scotia, announcing her visit to Ocean City and inviting me to spend some time with her at the new condo she had just purchased. Of course I accepted – I would never turn down a trip to the beach – and imagine my surprise and delight when it turned out that my cousin had purchased the very same apartment I had pinned up on my vision board!

Not only did I gain access to my dream vacation place – it was totally free and is now available to me any time I want in exchange for occasional cleaning and maintenance! I'll never again doubt the power of visualization!

Sandra W. of Orlando, FL thought it would be wonderful to have long hair:

As a little girl I had long hair, and it was beautiful and people used to touch it and compliment me about it. But long hair is impractical for my job as kindergarten teacher. The kids are always pulling my hair, and taking care of long hair takes too long in the mornings. I wanted extensions – just for the summer months when there is no school and I could pamper myself and take as much time to fuss with my hair as I want – all in the name of beauty.

Hair extensions are very expensive, and, frankly, I had no idea where I would get the money to buy them. Nevertheless, I decided to give manifesting a try. I was not sure what to focus on (money to buy them or the extensions themselves), but I knew that I had to be very clear on what I wanted – so ultimately I settled on the extensions. Visualizing myself with long hair was much easier than seeing a pile of money coming my way.

In May of last year I went to the Orlando Millennium Mall and visited a wig shop. I wanted to see what I looked like with long hair, and tried on wigs and had a friend take pictures of me. There was one picture I particularly liked, and I carried that one with me in my purse and looked at it ten times a day.

It was getting close to summer now, school would end soon and I still had short hair. I was getting more and more disappointed, already seeing my dream fading, when I remembered your instructions – you must believe with all your heart that you already have what you seek. So I took out my picture one more time and admired it, and that's when I heard a voice say behind me: " Wow, you look good with long hair, you should let it grow". I turned around and found myself talking to a complete stranger who happened to stand behind me in line for tickets to a movie.

We spent the next few minutes talking. Turns out that Michael was a hairdresser getting ready for a competition in Orlando for which he needed a willing model. I volunteered and did not only have long hair extensions for the summer but also the incredible experience of being the center of attention for one glorious night!

Whether your desires are big, like wanting a condo on the beach, or small like wanting long hair for the summer, when you put structures in place, trust in yourself and the universe, and apply the principles and suggestions outlined here, your wishes will come true.

For visualization techniques see Appendix C.

Go confidently in the direction of your dreams

Live the life you have imagined.

Henry David Thoreau

Chapter 8

Create The Life You Have Always Wanted

You've come a long way since you started reading this book. You have learned about your blueprint and how it has influenced your life and the lives of those around you. You now understand the role and power of your subconscious mind and you have learned how to communicate with it. You have taken a good look at your life and have re-discovered your passions, your talents and your values. You have written a new blueprint for yourself and you have put structures in place that will help you stay on your newfound path to a more fulfilled and happy life.

In this Chapter you will discover how to bring together all of these newfound wisdoms and create the life you have always wanted.

Abundance is your birthright

Did you know that you are born with the right to be a successful person? This knowledge seems to pass many people by, as they work in unfulfilling jobs and lead miserable lives. However, these people all have something in common. They take no initiative over controlling how the events of their lives will unfold.

One of the first commands ever documented as a rule for all of human kind to follow is to be fruitful and multiply. Well, we are still around and kicking, so multiplication is surely not the problem. Fruitfulness, however, can be seen as an issue.

While there are wildly successful individuals who are worth untold sums of money, they are few and far between. The average man doesn't have the kind of success that he deserves to have. Funny thing is, those who are successful were able to see their success before it happened. This foresight proves that success is achieved through the eyes of the beholder. Applying this to your own life is easier than you might think.

Enterprises that you may never have dreamed possible will open your eyes and enliven your true potential.

If you have trouble seeing yourself as a successful person, chances are that you will never taste the fruits and pleasures of the kind of lifestyle that a successful life brings. As you already know, the trick is to imagine and believe that you can be just as successful as anyone else. You must believe, in fact, that being abundant is your birthright.

Once you are able to understand and view your life in this manner, you will find that success will seemingly seek you out. Enterprises that you may never have dreamed possible will open your eyes and enliven your true potential. You will not only learn to enjoy the fruits of your labor, you will finally begin to feel that you actually deserve success. That is a feeling that is difficult to surpass.

Change your beliefs

Understanding this truism, you will quickly find that you must change the way that you think about your life if you are ever going to be able to make it in the big time. And there are a number of possible things that might require changing.

> First, attitude is a key element that most people must learn to adapt. Like I mentioned above, if you can't see it happening, it probably won't.

> Another thing you may have trouble changing is the way that you think about success. Success doesn't just come through large bank accounts, fast cars and big houses. These are merely things that successful people are able to purchase as products of their accomplishment.

> Success is a feeling of fulfillment in what makes up your life. Learning to change the ideas we have about success is difficult because society has ingrained traditional measures for success into our minds. This is why, in order to change your thinking, you must also change your beliefs.

Now, you might be thinking that changing your beliefs is far too drastic a step to take, even if the result is more success and happiness. However, it is possible to change your beliefs without jeopardizing the more personal areas of belief, such as religion and familial values.

We humans have beliefs about almost everything. When you take the time to analyze these beliefs, it becomes apparent that the vast majority of our convictions stem from the minds of other people. As you will recall from Chapter 1, we live by the blueprints of our parents, at least the first few years of our lives, until we are grown up ourselves. We inherit their customs, beliefs and attitudes toward life, and this means, in a nutshell, that we are investing ourselves and our lives in the theories and principles of other people.

Shouldn't we take the time to adapt a belief system that is dynamic enough to pertain specifically to our own unique lifestyle? After all, just as no two people define success by the same terms, no two people can be happy under the same circumstances. There are, however, universal ways to encourage you to develop your personal belief systems.

Success stems from positive thinking

Positive thinking is a barometer for understanding the overall capacity for human achievement. Nothing has ever been accomplished by negative, pessimistic thinking. The very idea behind a belief system, in all reality, is centered on understanding a positive way of seeing a situation. The more positive thoughts that enter any problem-solving situation, the more creative and reasonable ideas will follow.

The powers of positive thinking are applied every day from all different avenues of employment. Therapists use positive thinking and creative visualization in order to better help their patients overcome and take control over their lives. Businesses use positive thinking to maintain a presence as a continually growing enterprise, even when the going gets tough. This is how to succeed.

The overall fact of the matter is simply that positive results are attracted by positive thoughts. In other words, think positively and attract positive things in your life. These things can be both conceptual and tangible. You can increase your satisfaction with your marriage, relations with your co-workers or even boost your mood and energy levels. However, you can make a physical impact on your life through positive thinking as well.

Positive thinking is a barometer for understanding the overall capacity for human achievement.

You can refine your positive thinking to work through your actions in order to process them to your advantage. Your positive thinking can motivate you to increase the value of your house by doing repairs or putting on a new coat of paint. You can get a new job or a new car. All of the aspects and categories of your life are ripe for bettering through the application of positive, well meant thoughts. In turn, positive thinking will make an impact on those around you.

If this seems to you like repetition of what has been said in this book before – in fact, numerous times – it is on purpose. There is nothing more important than having a positive attitude toward anything that comes your way in life, and this is why I reemphasize this point over and over again until you get it.

Balance your Wheel of Life

The first step is to come to a good understanding of how your belief systems are working for you. What are the things that are most important to you? How do you interact with your schedule in order to put these preferred things in priority? Are you able to maintain these said things of preference as items of adequate attention? When you look at your belief system, how do you relate to the different areas of your life?

Being able to relate to all aspects of your life in a balanced way is as key to creating a connection to your happiness as is being able to relate equally to all of your emotions. If you are going to manage these priorities with any realistic attention, it is critical to understand exactly what they are.

When we look at how we use our intellect to guide us through our lives, we find that our attention and activities can be grouped into these areas:

➢ Family

➢ Work

➢ Money and finances

➢ Love and relationships

➢ Sexuality

➢ Religion and spirituality

➢ Social interactions

➢ The physical body

The easiest way to figure out how you divide your time and energy in these eight areas is to make a list of 10-20 important things you do daily. What areas, or aspects, of your life are covered in this list? Do certain areas dominate others?

For example, perhaps your list contains a number of items that are centered on things that supply you with short term happiness. These can be things such as television, sports, or even reading the news. If this is the case, you might consider re-evaluating the priorities for your list. Do you consider these things to offer you a true form of happiness? Probably not.

Other elements of your life are more concrete and can have more of an impact on achieving emotional changes. These can be things like family, work, money and finance, love and relationships, sexuality, spirituality and religion, social interactions, work and mental and social health. It is by understanding and maintaining a balance in these aspects of your life that your complete potential as a person will become unlocked.

Family

If you were to ask anyone what is their highest priority, there is a good probability that they would answer "family." Family ties have existed throughout the entire history of the human race. Family is the means by which we relate familiar feelings, sentiments and even tastes and preferences. It is with our families that we will blindly side and give our support, even in situations where we would turn our backs and close our eyes if the individual involved were a complete stranger.

It is with our families that we will blindly side and give our support

We are an incredibly social species, yet we base all of these social networks on the family environments into which we are born. Whether or not you agree, it is an undeniable truth that a great deal of our potential and options in life are partially determined by the families we are born into. The good thing is that this potential can grow.

By assuming that it is a totally healthy phenomenon to rely on and to be comforted by family situations, we are essentially saying that family is a good thing. What is important to understand about the previous statement, however, is what it doesn't say:

While a healthy family environment is a wonderful and helpful crutch, there are great numbers of individuals who are without this privilege. Some due to divorce, others death, and still others abandonment and neglect, many people lack the binding glue of a healthy family unit. To say that the absence of family is the absence of happiness would be to exclude countless individuals from being able to achieve their true potential.

However, this type of thinking is not relevant to the ideas that I am trying to express. Using the principles already discussed concerning happiness being available for anyone to achieve, it is better to understand that those without families must simply look to prioritizing other factors to help achieve their happiness.

If you are not concentrating on your family, you are probably hammering the hours away at the office. Or, you are taking time off from work to spend more time with your family. Either way one chooses to look at the situation, family and finances are tied at the hip eternally.

Work

The reasoning behind this thinking is simple. The entire purpose of holding a job is to provide for one's family. However, if you do not spend time working at your craft, you won't be able to make enough money to secure your family's happiness. In order to satisfy the greater goal, it is essential to learn how to balance these two elements of the equation. The easiest way to understand how to do this is to create and understand a correct value for money and finances.

Work is an essential element for your happiness. It is not only necessary to provide the means for food and shelter and to put your children through college – it is much more. Work gives you purpose, a feeling of accomplishment, it motivates you, it channels your creativity, it structures your day and it is the backbone of all that has ever been created by mankind. Without work – someone's work – there would be no world as we know it today.

The key to your happiness is to find the right kind of work and to balance work time with the other things you could be using your time on. Standards for a work day and work week have been established throughout the world, and of course, they vary from region to region and for each sector. Agricultural work differs greatly from industrial, where shifts are common, and these differ from office work and housework. Whatever your line of work, the number of hours you spend working should be proportionate to the hours needed to relax, spend with family and friends, and to keep you healthy in body, soul and spirit.

Money and finances

Money and finances are not commodities. They are not symbols of wealth or prosperity; rather, money is paper and metal. It is the value that we attach to these items that make them desirable. What makes them functional is their ability to easily and conveniently convert themselves into things of sustenance. This can easily lead people to make the mistake of associating money with happiness.

Money can, in fact, purchase items which can provide you with temporary peace and tranquility. A brand new television set might make the problems you are having with the other aspects of your life seem to vanish. However, just as the television set will eventually become dated and obsolete technology, its effect on your overall happiness will also eventually fade. The trick, then, is using money and finances to provide a lasting happiness.

Love and relationships

Of all of the things that further the idea that happiness is something that can be found, love is perhaps the most relevant. When you meet someone who gets you, who truly understands and cares about you, it seems like all problems become null and void. The blissful ride of love's first and finest moments is like a cure-all drug with an endless supply of happiness. Confidence that you never knew you had comes bubbling to the surface when you are with that special someone. Surely, you feel like you are the person you have the potential to be. That is, until the infatuation wears off and reality sets in. Sure, the people we love can have lasting effects on our happiness and well being. However, like all of these aspects of happiness, love must be managed.

...like all of these aspects of happiness, love must be managed.

Understanding infatuation is the first step to understanding how to manage love and relationships. An infatuated person can be a confident, passionate and enlightened individual. However, they can also be a foolish one. Like everything in life, love comes with its pluses and minuses.

One of the most obvious negatives is that the happiness of just one person is no longer the goal. What satisfies one person's needs in terms of happiness might make another individual miserable. The idea of teamwork can complicate the process of unlocking a person's potential. However, this should not make love seem as something to be avoided. In addition to activating some aspects of happiness that arguably cannot be attained through any other means, love enables a deeper development of a person's potential. Helping someone realize who they are meant to be can help you along on your own journey.

Sexuality

One of the make or break aspects of many relationships is the element of human sexuality. On one hand, sexuality is a procreative tool, something to aid in the transferring of the strengths and charms of one generation on to the next. It is an unfailing system of reproduction that enables the great dream and potential of the human species to continue on this planet. However, sexuality can also be a wonderful experience that can be shared between individuals. Sexuality is an identity, a sense of purpose and a unique separating factor between you and everyone else. When both of these aspects of sexuality's magical power are combined through an act of love, the results can be a happiness that extends throughout many different levels.

When examining sexuality at an individual level, it helps to understand that there are no specific rules or regulations for understanding and categorizing such a phenomenon. It is important to understand your own sexuality in order to respect the sexuality of others. The greatest lesson to learn about sexuality is really a simple lesson of respect and understanding.

While sexuality can allow for a great amount of potential to be discovered through one's own self, there is just as much and perhaps even more to be learned about those around you. As long as you are able to make yourself open to understanding, you will find that a healthy sexual self-awareness and tolerance will do wonders for your overall development as a human being.

Many people frown at the main concept of this ideology because they feel they must abandon their own in order to adopt it. By no means is this the case. The idea of changing your belief system, as previously mentioned, is in no way related to a rejection of any philosophical or religious beliefs. It is simply an act of re–categorizing how these beliefs function for you in your own life.

Religion and spirituality

Religion has been around for as long as human kind has graced the earth. On the merit of its longevity alone, it simply cannot be argued that religion does not belong in our quest for happiness. In fact, it was through religion alone that many people have claimed to have found themselves for the first time. These born-again believers are not across the board representatives of all of humanity. However, lessons can be learned from their experiences with respect to a method of incorporating religion into your life.

Much like handling the sexuality of yourself and others, the most important thing to consider is tolerance and understanding. It is crucial to allow religion into your life as an enlightening and pacifying tool.

What is not acceptable or helpful is allowing religion to become a divisive and disruptive element. Fanatical religious experiments not only create a negative thought process for both parties involved, they separate people from each other. Happiness is achieved through peace and tranquility: not divisiveness and disunity. Therefore, religion, like sexuality, should be engaged by a unique approach that changes on a person to person basis.

Social interactions

Both religious experiences and human sexuality are covered in the realm of understanding human social interactions. As with family interactions, the social webs that are woven through communications and human contact can be quite comforting during times of duress. We use these relationships, sometimes in place of our families, to create a crutch for hostile environments. These can be incredibly healthy and helpful scenarios.

Keeping healthy social contacts is a great way to gain an inner channel to your own happiness. What is necessary to avoid, however, is using the crutch that these networks can provide exclusively. Like most of the topics which are covered here, it is important to take a moderate approach to implementing them in your life. Even the most outgoing individuals will be faced with time alone during which they must accomplish things.

If you become too reliant on your social connections, you will be unable to function alone. This can be especially dangerous for getting the most out of the opportunities that you are dealt in life. If a great opportunity were to arise that might require moving, say a job opening overseas, a socially dependent person might be reluctant to leave the safety of their web for the unknown. This reveals that, although the individual may seem strong in their group, familiar setting, they are not comfortable with themselves or confident.

The physical body

While most of the categories of your beliefs and structures mentioned thus far are things which can be controlled directly by each of us, health is an aspect of our happiness that can be variable. We can put ourselves in the best situations and still succumb to mental and physical health deterioration. These can be devastating to a person who is not well prepared to deal with them.

In order to live a fulfilling life that matches your potential, you must be able to handle even the hardest curve ball that life might throw at you. Physical health ailments are probably more variable to prevent and can come randomly or because of your gene pool. However, there are many things that you can do to be prepared as best as you could to handle what may come.

First of all, regularly seeing your physician and other professional specialists is a great habit for ensuring a lifetime of happiness. Imagine that your body is a car. You would take your car in for all of the necessary repairs, fill it with fuel when needed, and perform all of the scheduled maintenance repairs. Just as you would do for your ride, you should do for your body.

> We can put ourselves in the best situations and still succumb to mental and physical health deterioration.

While the physical ailments of the body might be easier to understand than mental issues, it is the mental issues that can to a greater extent rob us of our happiness and contentment. After all, a mental condition is in all reality a malfunction by our body's ability to perceive what makes us happy. You could be in the most serene and peaceful environment and be devoid of all happiness and feeling; that is if your mental health is not up to par.

The steps to preserving your mental health are not all that different than the steps outlined here for achieving your inner happiness and becoming the best you that you can be. Keeping healthy company and regulating and managing all of the different belief elements of your life is one way to help prepare your mind to remain in a healthy state.

In addition to this, health practices such as yoga, meditation, Pilates and virtually any regular cardiovascular exercise can do wonders toward achieving this goal. These eight areas discussed above are like spokes of the wheel that carries us through life. If these spokes are not balanced, if they are not of equal length, this wheel would not give us a very smooth ride at all.

Let's do an exercise to drive in this point:

Take a few minutes to think about how satisfied you are with your performance today in each of the categories above. For example, ask yourself these questions in the area of:

> Family: Are you spending enough time with your family? Are you supportive of your spouse and children? Are there issues that need to be resolved? How satisfied are you with your family relationships? Could you do better in this area?

> Work: How do you feel about your work? Do you love it, hate it? How good are you at it? Do you like your co-workers? How about your boss? Are you dreaming of a different career? Are you ready to retire?

> Money and finances: Are you earning enough money to support your family? What are your spending habits? Do you splurge all the time or save too much? Are you investing for your future and the future of your children?

> Love and love relationships: Are you open to love someone and to accept love from someone? Do your love relationships last? Are you scared or open to let someone into your heart and soul? Do you share your innermost secrets with someone special? How satisfied are you with your love relationships?

> Sexuality: Are you in harmony with your sexuality? Are you sexually active and are you satisfied with your sex life? If not, would you like to be? Are you comfortable with the frequency of your sexual activity?

➤ Religion and spirituality: Do you feel connected to a higher power? What is your relationship with this entity? Are you satisfied with your spiritual life or do you have unanswered questions that keep you from fully embracing your faith?

➤ Social interactions: Do you have close friends whom you can rely on when you need someone to talk to? Do you easily interact with other people? Are you shy or outgoing? Is there something in your social interactions that you would like to change?

➤ Your physical body: Are you satisfied with the way your body looks and with your overall health? Do you think you could lose a few pounds? Are you exercising regularly? How is your overall health? Are you eating right and feeding your body proper nutrition? Are you drinking too much alcohol?

For each category, assign a percentage level of satisfaction from 10% to 100%, and then enter these in the Wheel of Life. For our example, let us assume that you have assessed yourself the following values for each category:

Family relations 60%

Money and finances 50%

Work 70%

Love relationships 40%

Sexuality...80%

Spirituality..60%

Social relations...70%

Physical body..85%

When we enter these values in the Wheel of Life, this is what it looks like. Instead of shortening the spokes of this wheel to correspond to the percentage values you have indicated, we'll simply fill in the spaces between the spokes and get this picture:

The Wheel Of Life

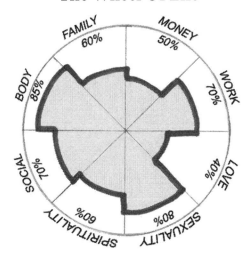

Now imagine this wheel, the way it is depicted above, as one of the wheels of your bicycle. What kind of ride would you experience? Would it be smooth and comfortable? Hardly! You would be jolted up and down and become tired in no time at all. Your wheel would not last long either, as some parts never touch the ground while others take the full beating. The best you could do with this wheel is to get off it and push it along beside you...

And this is what happens in real life when your Wheel of Life is not balanced. Instead of riding and living your life to the fullest, you have to get off and shuffle alongside this rattling wheel, which represents your personal world.

Isn't it time to make some changes in your life?

Once you have outlined and come to understand these elements that make up the total experience of your life, the task at hand is to make the necessary changes. The best thing for most people is to put new structures in place for maintaining the balance throughout these elements. These structures can be as simple as creating a new schedule. They can be as complicated as relocating and finding a new job, reconsidering a negative relationship, spending more time at work and less time hanging out with friends (or vice versa) or any number of combinations.

The trick is to come up with a way to implement these changes over the entire range of your life in a method that will allow you to continue them. Think of it as a diet. All of the good, proven diets target not only the actual food intake management, they seek to disrupt the harmful behaviors and influences that lead to bad eating habits. If a diet doesn't address the fact that you go out every weekend and eat a lot of junk, the diet probably won't work. In much the same way, if you are unable to come up with a consistent way to work these solutions into your life, the changes you are able to make probably won't last.

Creating a structure for implementing these types of changes can be a bit of a challenge. Working them in slowly and one at a time is a good way to ensure that you do not become overwhelmed and abandon your project completely. It also helps to not lose sight of the overall goal: achieving happiness and becoming a better you. If the act of achieving this goal is becoming stressful or negatively impacting your life, slow down.

Everyone feels some pressure and encounters difficulties when making substantial changes.

All of these structures will be around to work into your life tomorrow or, if necessary, later on down the road. Don't look at this as laziness or even procrastination. Rather, understand that it took a great deal of time to shape who you are as a person now. Likewise, it will take a while to remold and restructure you into this new and wonderful person you want to be.

Work with an accountability coach

If you are finding that implementing these changes on your own is too difficult a task, there are other options for achieving your goals. First of all, understand that no one is able to instantly make these kinds of life changing adjustments without flinching.

Everyone feels some pressure and encounters difficulties when making substantial changes. An accountability coach is a way to help you reach the goals. Much in the same way as a personal trainer keeps you on your toes when it comes to a workout, an accountability coach will keep your lifestyle changes on target. These individuals are often trained over a wide variety of disciplines and can be found for almost any budget.

In addition, if you are unable to afford an actual accountability coach, you might consider asking a friend or family member to sit in for the role for you. After all, it is sometimes not just the training but having another person at your side, believing in you, that makes the difference. When you know that someone else is as concerned with your overall well being as you are, you can go the extra yard.

Also, as with most things in life, the hardest part can be to simply get started. After you start, every day will be increasingly easier, since the first days are the hardest. Perhaps you need that trainer to get you out of bed for the first few weeks of your new workout regime. However, by the third or fourth month, you will be working effectively on your own, trusting your own discipline.

Set your goals

One of the first things that either a personal trainer or an accountability coach will tell you is to set goals. Not only is it important to set goals, it is important to refer back to them often. If you are a mountain climber and there is a big rock that you are currently working on, you will most likely fail if you try to tackle the thing in its entirety on your first or second try. The best strategy is to take it down, little by little.

But how are you able to make sure that you are still making progress each and every day? The trick is to push yourself a little bit further each and every time you head out. By setting goals like this, you are able to break down a large obstacle into a more manageable set of pieces. Once you establish your goals, or pieces, place them somewhere where they will not easily become forgotten.

Many a great idea fails because of poor execution. Perhaps in the case of the mountain climber, he has a great plan that will get him to the top of the mountain in one month's time. However, he must follow the plan regularly if he is able to achieve his goal. Furthermore, for every day that he does not do his part to reaching this goal, he will fall back a little. If he does not place his plan or goals somewhere where he will see them and be influenced by them every day, the odds that he will achieve his final goal are slim.

Write down your goals

When you figure out your goals for making yourself a better person, write them out clearly and concisely. Writing down the goals serves several important purposes. First, it causes you to use more of your senses. By writing down the goal you get the physical touch of your hand guiding the pen and forming the words on the paper and you get the visual of seeing your goal written down. Then,

By setting goals like this, you are able to break down a large obstacle into a more manageable set of pieces.

you have to form an internal dialogue about the goal in order to translate it into words on paper. Just by writing down your goals, you have accomplished 2 of the 3 steps necessary to affect your subconscious mind.

Next, you need to add the emotion to this equation. You must imagine yourself actually achieving the goal you have written down and allow yourself to feel the positive emotions that would come from that. It is absolutely vital that you imagine your success in the present tense and experience the emotion as if it were real right now. If you imagine it in the future, even though you might get a pleasant emotion from it, it will always remain out there in the future. Your subconscious will allow it to stay there and believe that good feelings are derived just from the dreaming of the goal, rather than from achieving it.

After you have written down your goals, make several copies of your plan. Place one of these copies in your bedroom. Perhaps another might go in your wallet. You could put one of these up at your office or work place. Even better yet, you can give copies of your plan to people who are working with you to achieve your goals. If they know what you are trying to achieve and the manner by which you are aiming, they will be able to help you make the best decisions possible to get to your finish line. If your friends are the reason that you go out every weekend and eat poorly when with them, maybe they will change their habits if they know what your aim is.

Start having fun

After you have begun to implement your goals and new plan, the real fun starts to happen. Since it can be easy to get caught up in all of the technical speak and step by step processes, you might forget that what you are after is as natural as breathing and as simple as sleep. It's not possible to review the ultimate message too frequently: happiness is inside of you.

While all of the methods and plans are necessary, the final thing that you are reaching for is a way to live a better life. The only way to successfully achieve this is by actually going out and living your life. In addition to being the final goal of this program, it is the only way to test and see if the changes that you are making are working. There is not a single clear answer for each and every one of us. You must tailor all of these suggestions to fit you: your lifestyle, your situation. If what you are doing is not making you happy, than it is not going to work: try something else.

When you finally are able to experience the first exhilarating rush of happiness that is sourced from within, you will feel like a totally new person. There is a reason for that: you are! You will find that you are more agreeable to the people that you meet and interact with. You will be more energized and you will feel that your life has a deeper and greater meaning. You will not have lost touch with the beliefs and values that you held dear before you enacted these changes.

On the contrary, you will be closer and truer to them than you ever were before. The greatest part of this is the even deeper satisfaction you will gain from the knowledge that all of these changes that occurred came from within your own heart. Once you learn that you have the power to control your emotions from within, you can start to do truly amazing things.

In the event that you have a slip up or have a bad day, you must remember the nature of happiness. Part of what makes it so wonderful is how it works in tandem with the down times. If you are unable to get through a little rough patch, then chances are that you still have some work to do. The idea behind becoming the best you that you can be is to be stable throughout all the range of your emotional responses. The idea is to learn to control all of your human responses to situations. If you find that you are not being as happy as often as you would like, there is one more thing you can try. Be happy just for the sake of being happy.

Be happy just for the sake of being happy.

Be happy and enjoy a happier life!

While it would seem only logical that those who have less-than-satisfactory lives are generally less-than-happy, the fact is that there are plenty of people who have wonderful lives, yet are no happier than their unfortunate counterparts. If what you have in life is not the deciding factor in how happy you are, then what is the deciding factor? What makes some people happy, while others are not?

The most important key in happiness can be found in one word: yourself! You could have every material possession, every opportunity, everything good in life, but being happy with yourself first determines how much you will enjoy and appreciate everything else.

If you did not realize this before now, you may have no idea where to begin. Regardless of how well or little you think of yourself, feel about yourself, and relate to yourself, the essential component in being happy with yourself is to begin by eliminating the nega-

CHAPTER 8 - CREATE THE LIFE YOU ALWAYS WANTED

tives. When you start defining yourself in positive terms that suit you now, you will begin to be much happier with yourself. You no longer need someone else to tell you who you are, what you are, or what you are capable of becoming or doing - you will have these matters in your own hands.

Happiness exists within all of us

One of the reasons that positive thinking can have such an impact on us is that we almost seem to gravitate toward a happy solution, provided one is available and in sight. This is because for all people (regardless of race, age, creed, social status or disability), happiness exists within all of us.

Understanding this principle is a key change in belief, but doing so will open a world of wonderful possibilities to you. Understanding happiness is truly key to becoming the person that you wish you were. It is a way of unlocking the limitless and unfailing potential that each one of us possesses. So, in order to better accomplish this enlightenment, it helps to have a firm grasp of what happiness truly is.

Happiness exists in all of us. Well, you might ask, why is there so much unhappiness throughout the world? Why are there deep concentrations of pain and suffering and small pockets of blissful enjoyment? It's because happiness is a great and overwhelming feeling that leaves little time (or perceived need) for understanding where it came from. For unhappy people, the problem is equally simple: they look to seek out happiness. These individuals will travel around and change a great number of variables in their lives in order to come across happiness. It is only once they have the capacity for happiness within their own control that they will be able to unlock it.

Understanding happiness is truly key to becoming the person that you wish you were.

Unlock the happiness within you

Once you have established that you are ultimately the source of your own happiness, it is time to learn how to unlock it. Like most good things in life, happiness is not guaranteed, nor is it constant. It is remembering the lessons that you learned throughout the sad times that make happiness seem ever sweeter when it is achieved. And, although a life time of pure and unflinching happiness is quite unlikely, you can take measures to maximize the amount of happy times that you do have.

One way to ensure this is to understand and appreciate the whole range of human emotions. By better appreciating the bad times, the good times will seem that much more valuable. Once you are able to achieve this balance, you are ready to understand the greater ways of unlocking your internal happiness.

By better appreciating the bad times, the good times will seem that much more valuable.

Look at the situations which make you upset; they are generally stressful and disruptive scenarios. On the contrary, happy times are full of peace and tranquility.

In order to achieve your happiness from within, peace and relaxation are the ultimate goals. For thousands of years in eastern philosophies, utilizing the principles of peace and relaxation are tantamount to achieving the various levels of contentment. Many of these beliefs are centered on the idea that a mind at peace is a happy mind.

The desire to be happy is a universal part of human nature

There are nearly as many definitions for the word "happiness" as there are human beings on this planet. Every person has his or her own unique definition of what happiness means; this is because each person has his or her own unique desires, wishes, thoughts, emotions and dreams.

You want to be happy. You want your life to be brimming with happiness – to enjoy, and to share with others. The first thing you must do in order to make happiness a part of your everyday life and a part of your future is to decide what it means to you.

If you "compare notes" with your friends, or even with your family members, you may go off track, and you may be quite disappointed. As they, too, are individuals, you cannot reasonably expect them to describe happiness in precisely the same manner as you do for yourself. When you are planning to make happiness a part of your life, putting the focus on your own definition first is essential. After all, it is quite impossible to attain something if you are uncertain as to what it is that you wish to attain.

There are three basic approaches to the subject happiness. Some people have an external approach. To these people, the existence or absence of happiness is primarily determined by what they have, what they do, what they accomplish. They find the prospect of a nice family vacation, a new job promotion or opportunity, or similar types of external factors to be happiness.

Others take an internal approach. For them, the highest and best state of happiness involves a true sense of inner-peace, contentment, and general well-being. Still others take the approach that true happiness is about acceptance – that everything is fine exactly as it is. Individual personality traits account for differences in happiness styles – and knowing what happiness means to you is the surest way that you can attain it.

...knowing what happiness means to you is the surest way that you can attain it. When you know what happiness means to you, you can then proceed toward it by beginning to remove the obstacles. Whether a new home is your fondest desire, whether you wish to have a sense of contentment in your everyday life, or whether you feel that you are relatively happy with yourself and your life but simply need to be sure that you are on the right track... happiness does not need to be a far-off goal that you may or may not reach someday -- it is something that is within reach right now.

Decide what happiness means to you – and what you reach for will be within your grasp!

Be happy without reason

To be happy without reason is to truly enjoy the spontaneity of life. The spice of life is variety and variety manifests itself through a rejection of the routine every now and then. Yes, keeping schedules and setting goals are important.

However, every now and then it is nice to just simply kick back and be happy to be alive. Be happy that it is spring, if it is spring. If it is winter, be happy for snowballs and holiday greetings. In other words, find something about a situation that makes you happy. Make yourself be happy about the mundane and ordinary. If you are able to do this, you have truly unlocked the key to being in control of your happiness.

⌣

The ideas and theories expressed here address how to make yourself fruitful and happy under your own hand and through self sufficiency. What is wonderful about this is that you will also possess the ability to pass the happiness on to your following generations. As you create life, your attitude will be reflected in the behavior of your offspring.

Happiness is a concept that is learned, and once it is learned it can't be unlearned. Everyone knows the classic example of riding a bike. Once you pick it up, it doesn't matter how much time goes by, you'll always know how to ride. Well, the reason is that our mind expands over a concept and never turns back.

Once you realize how something works, it is built in to your universal understanding of everything around you. So, once you have discovered how you can be happy with yourself, you won't ever be looking for it again.

Conclusion

In this book I have presented fundamental concepts that will lead you to a happier and more fulfilled life if you allow yourself to be guided. Take a few minutes to review these eight essential steps toward getting rid of negative blueprints from the past and replacing them with positive new structures.

Get ready to step into a great new life that you create yourself. Keep in mind that:

1. Everyone lives by a blueprint – there is no exception to this rule.

2. You must understand that this blueprint that defines and channels your life, also influences the people around you. If you care about them you will want to examine your blueprint and change those aspects of it that are not conducive to their happiness.

3. Your blueprint resides in your subconscious mind; you must understand how it works and how you can communicate with it if you want to succeed in reprinting your blueprint. You have the power to do this!

4. Since your blueprint was created when you were a small child, you must go back in time to discover the very moment when it was formed. You do this by quieting your conscious mind through deep relaxation or meditation and allowing your subconscious mind to show you the way.

5. Many techniques are available to you to deal with the emotional stress you might feel when you discover your blueprint. Practice these techniques on an ongoing basis to learn how to communicate effectively with your subconscious mind.

6. When you are ready to Reprint Your Blueprint, find your passion first, rethink your values and listen to your inner voices. Now is the time to consciously and purposefully define your life's path, and do it your way!

7. Create new structures in your life that will support you as you rebuild your life based on your New Blueprint. The old structures no longer serve you. Surround yourself with people you trust, change your attitude, be grateful for what you already have and first and foremost, love yourself!

8. With your new blueprint and the new structures in place, you can create the life you have always wanted. Change your beliefs and understand that abundance is your birthright. Balance your Wheel of Life, set your goals and start having fun! Be happy and enjoy a happier and more fulfilled life!

Start today. Make your life into what you truly want it to be.

∽

Change is the law of life. And those who look only to the past or present are certain to miss the future.

John F. Kennedy

∽

〜

"Every journey starts with the first step"

Lao Tzu

〜

You have triumphed in taking the first step of your personal journey to fulfillment and happiness by simply reading this book. If you would like to take the next step, I would be happy to accompany you on your journey by offering you a variety of tools that will assist you in reaching your goals. These tools can be found online at www.AndreaLucas.com

My objective in writing this book was to share my understanding of the power of the blueprint that rules our lives and to make a system available to you by which you can erase your old blueprint and Reprint Your Blueprint to one that brings you the happiness you want and deserve. I am open to any and all suggestions on how to improve this system so YOU will realize your dreams.

Please send your comments and suggestions to

Andrea@AndreaLucas.com.

Appendices

Appendix A

RELAXATION TECHNIQUES

Why is it so important to learn how to relax your body and mind? Well, if you have ever experienced any of these symptoms below, then you know what stress feels like – and stress is the principle cause of many debilitating illnesses of our time:

➢ Back pain, tightness around your shoulder blades and neck area

➢ Shortness of breath, huffing and puffing going up the stairs

➢ Panic attacks

➢ Snapping at loved ones

➢ Being irritable and having mood swings

➢ Worrying about everything

➢ Inability to fall asleep

➢ Restlessness

➢ Grinding your teeth, just to mention a few…

On the other hand, have you ever been to the beach, or sitting at the water's edge at a lake, basking in the sun, worry free and enjoying the tranquility and peace all around you? Imagine yourself in that place right now – eyes closed, feel the gentle breeze caress your body, the sunshine kiss your skin and listen to the waves roll on shore, and to the songs of the birds in the trees. You are totally relaxed and your mind is empty of conscious thought; you enter into a dream state – you might even fall asleep for a while – and when you are ready, you arouse from this state fully refreshed and energized.

Which feeling to you prefer?

It does not take much imagination to guess your answer. Of course, the relaxed state of the body and mind is more desirable. So, you have a choice: since it is not possible for two opposites to exist at the same time – you cannot be relaxed and stressed at the same time – which state do you choose?

Learning how to relax is not difficult. To start,

1. Shake your body, shake your arms, roll your head from one side to the other and even jump a little to physically invoke a change in the way you feel.

2. Sit down in a comfortable chair or stretch out on your bed or sofa, as it is not easy to do this exercise while standing up. This is not to say however that you have to be in a quiet place, or in a special room. You can do a relaxation exercise anywhere, even in the office while sitting at your desk.

3. The next step involves the breath. When I first started these exercises I could not understand why I should re-place my usual shallow breaths with deep breaths from the belly that move the diaphragm, but now I under-stand: the breath carries the most important nourish-ment – oxygen – to every cell of the body. We can live over one month without food, perhaps ten days without water, but not five minutes without oxygen.

4. So breathe deeply, and imagine that you are taking in goodness and health with every breath in, and that you are expelling stress, anger, anxieties and all negative thoughts with every breath out.

5. Now begin to purposely move, wiggle, rotate, stretch, lift or contract each body part, one at a time, beginning with your feet and moving up to your head and face.

This is a slow process which has the purpose of making you aware of each body part so you can release the tension in it. Do this:

- Wiggle your toes and lift them up, feeling and stretching them.

- Rotate your ankles several times, lift your feet off the floor or bed a few inches, and then let them fall back, totally relaxed. If you prefer, you can do this one foot at a time.

- Continue to tense your calf muscles, feel the tension in them – and then let go.

- Now tighten your thigh muscles. This might involve your quadriceps, hamstrings as well as your glutes (gluteus maximus in your buttocks). Crunch these muscles tightly, hold the crunch, and then let go, feeling the tension dissipate and leaving the muscles limp and loose.

- Move up your body by tightening your stomach muscles, pressing against the diaphragm, pushing as you would for a bowel movement, feel the tension, then let go.

- Now make a tight fist and release it. Tighten your biceps, lift your arms a few inches, then let them drop again. Do this one arm at a time, saying to yourself: my arm is heavy, my muscles are warm and heavy.

- Crunch your shoulder blades together, tighten your back muscles as tight as you can, hold your breath and count to six; then breathe out and relax your shoulders and back.

- Repeat this for the muscles of your neck. Say to yourself: the relaxing power is moving up my spine, relaxing every fiber of my being; it is now moving up the back of my neck, relaxing my neck, and up my scalp and relaxing my scalp. Feel your neck and scalp relax and feel the tension go.

• Now allow the relaxing power to flow down your face, relaxing your forehead, and relaxing the muscles around your eyes. Allow a little space between your teeth and relax your jaws. Feel the tension drain from your face, open your mouth slightly and take another deep breath, exhaling through your mouth.

• By now you feel totally relaxed and at ease, with all your muscles being limp and loose, limp and loose. Your entire body feels warm and heavy and you are enjoying this blissful state of relaxation. When it is time to leave this wonderful state, you feel refreshed and ready to go on with your day. Your senses are sharp, your mind is clear and you perform at a heightened state of alertness.

What a great way to start, continue or end your day!

This technique is called "progressive muscle relaxation", and, as you can see, it's very simple to do and everyone can learn it without any difficulty. The two other major types of relaxation techniques are

➤ **Autogenic training**, where a combination of visualization and body awareness is used to bring someone to deep relaxation. For example, you first imagine a wonderful place, like the beach, or any other place where you feel safe and comfortable. Then you focus on the different parts of your body and feel heaviness or warmth in each body part, relaxing it as you mentally move from one to the other.

➤ **Meditation**. We will discuss meditation separately. It is interesting to note that meditation requires the body to be relaxed first before the mind can move into the intuitive state which is the desired meditative state.

The two most popular forms of meditation in the U.S. are Transcendental Meditation where you repeat a mantra to relax your mind; and mindfulness meditation, where you focus your attention on the sensations and random thoughts you are experiencing.

Other relaxation methods:

When you do not have time to do the full progressive muscle relaxation method described above, partial relaxation techniques and massaging of your body and body parts will help relieve tension:

> ➤ A shoulder and neck massage can reduce muscle tension in these parts of your body and make you feel like new again. This will require another person to give you the massage, and you can then reciprocate.

> ➤ Knead the muscles on the side of the neck (the Trapezius muscles) with your thumbs and work on the back of the neck. Move your fingers and thumbs in circles, using first light pressure and increasing it when you feel any muscle spasms in your partner's back. Press your thumbs into the muscles and knead the upper back and shoulders. Use long strokes with your hands from the neck to the shoulders when you are finished with the neck and shoulder massage. Your partner will be ecstatic!

> ➤ Massage your face starting with the forehead. Gently move your fingers from the center of your forehead to the temples; gently pull the hair around your face at the roots; massage your nose and along the rim of your ears; tap ever so lightly around your eyes; circle your mouth with your fingers and stroke your neck, stretching it in all directions; raise your eyebrows; grin from side to side; roll your eyes and make funny faces. You'll love this exercise, and so will your face! When you're done, you'll have rosy cheeks and a healthy, fresh complexion!

> ➤ Foot massage: for me, there is nothing more relaxing than a gentle foot massage. I have very sensitive feet and the hard pressure of reflexology does not do me any good, so I go for the kinder, gentler massage of my ankles, soles, arches and toes. You can do this massage yourself, but it's best if done by someone else – even a pedicurist will do a good job (if tipped accordingly...)

➤ If you can stand the reflexology pressure, by all means – go for it. There are over 7,000 nerve endings in each foot, and these nerve endings are linked to all the organs of your body. A tender spot on the sole of your foot tells the reflexologist where there is potential trouble in one of your body's organs.

➤ A full-body massage is bliss of course any time; there are numerous types of massage available anywhere, the most common of which are these:

• Swedish massage: the massage therapist uses massage oil and works it into the muscles with long, soothing strokes and circular movements.

• Aromatherapy massage: this type of massage is similar to the Swedish massage, except that the therapist uses aromatic oils, also known as essential oils. Most commonly used is lavender, an essential oil that is known to alleviate stress. Other oils in this category include chamomile, fir, rose, sandalwood, geranium, etc.

• Shiatsu massage: this is a Japanese massage technique where the therapist massages the acupressure points along the spine. This massage is very relaxing and does not cause sore muscles, as might be the case with a deep tissue massage.

• Deep tissue massage: I get this type of massage at my chiropractor's office. The therapist puts enormous pressure on my back moving against the grain of the muscles and his thumbs work on knots until they are gone and the muscles are soft and supple again. I am sore for a couple of days after this massage, but that's a different, much more sustainable pain than the constant, sharp and cramping pain of the stress knots in my back.

• Hot stone massage is not something I have experienced, but I'm told that it is soothing and relaxing.

Hot stones are placed on the body and sometimes the therapist uses the stones to gently massage the back. This type of massage is recommended for those who prefer a lighter touch.

• And sports massage: this massage is used to loosen the muscles and prevent injury in persons who are athletically active. This is actually not a very relaxing massage but quite useful if you are stiff and need to work on your flexibility.

Appendix B

LEARN HOW TO MEDITATE

Meditation is a very simple process that is best learned by yourself. This process involves three stages and seven keys, which are explained below.

First, let us explore the three states of the mind we can find ourselves in. There is the

> **Superficial state** that tends to occupy our mind most of the time. This is where our thoughts are racing a mile a minute, where they jump from one subject to the other, where little attention is given to any one of the thoughts that come to mind. For example, you see a red car racing by out of the corner of your eyes; that triggers a thought of a friend you have who owns such a car; you recall a drive you took with him one time; you remember the place you stopped to have a couple of beers; and then the nice girl you saw at the bar and asked out for a date; and then you wonder whatever happened to her... moments later another impression enters your mind through one of your five senses and another series of thoughts begin their dance through your mind.

> When you are in this state, you cannot concentrate and are easily distracted. None of these random thoughts have any relevance of who you really are.

> **Analytical state** where you concentrate and focus on one thing at a time and perform your deeper, analytical thinking. When you are in this state of the mind, great achievements are possible, whether these are learning to tie your shoe laces, passing the SAT test, winning a race, writing a book or solving difficult mathematical

problems. The deepest level of conscious thought is the analytical level.

➤ And the **Intuitive state** where thinking stops and intuition takes over. When you experience something intuitively, you never forget it. Creativity is born in this intuitive state, when you put your pencil to paper or your brush to the canvas and simply know what to write or paint and when it is perfect. This is when your real self reveals itself.

So, when you meditate, you want to move your mind from the first stage through the second to the third, the level of intuition. You start by paying attention to the random thoughts in your mind; you concentrate on one thing only, such as an object, a sound or a mantra, and you purposefully brush the random thoughts away; and you repeat this process until your intuitive mind takes over all by itself and you meditate.

Meditation is not limited to an indoor experience. With practice, you can learn to move your mind through these three stages very quickly, to the point where the outside world disappears at an instance and you find yourself in the deepest refreshing meditative state no matter where you are. My niece practices meditation regularly – in the NY subway!

Five Principles of Meditation

For the beginners, however, I suggest that you proceed with the five principles of meditation that will make you a pro in no time and greatly enhance your experience:

1. Find a quite place and make it your meditation "room". If you have a separate room that would be great, but there is no need for it. You can easily use a corner of your bedroom or living room, for as long as your privacy will be assured in that space when you want to meditate. No disturbance please during your private time.

Prepare this space for your meditation. Get a large pillow to sit on if you are comfortable sitting on the floor, otherwise select a comfortable chair, and make sure you have a small table handy where you can place your meditation candle, or incense if you like, or your iPod or CD player for your choice of music.

2. As you have prepared your meditation space, so you must prepare your physical body for the experience of meditation. You can accomplish this by changing into comfortable clothes, taking off your shoes, taking a bath if you have time, or simply washing your hands and face.

3. When you are ready to begin your meditation, light your candle and incense, play your favorite meditation music softly and sit on your pillow or in your chair. Do not lie down on the bed or in a reclining chair, as this could lead to sleep – and you don't want to sleep now. You want to concentrate. So sit straight, place your hands on you lap and look into the flame or your chosen object. Do not stare at it with sharp focused eyes. Instead, relax your eyes, lower your lids a bit and let the light diffuse around your meditation object.

Relax your body. For a minute or two, perform one of the relaxation methods described in Appendix A until you feel all the tension drain from your body. Start your meditation by taking six deep, cleansing breaths and focus on within. Brush away all extraneous thoughts. When noises intrude from the outside, repeat your mantra to yourself and when you concentrate on doing just that, these noises will fade into the background.

Your mantra can be a word, a phrase that has meaning, or just some sounds that have no meaning but are pleasant to the ears. Your rhythmic breathing could be your mantra, your heart beat another. When you become accomplished in meditation, you will hear the universal sound of vibration, the "ohmmmmmm" sound which is the most soothing sound you will ever hear in your life. Until then, you can emulate this sound by voicing it yourself in a soft and gentle voice.

4. When you first start to meditate, try not to overdo it. Sitting on a pillow may cramp your legs at first, or trying too hard to concentrate and not succeeding might deter you from trying again. So, take your time in learning the proper techniques of meditation and start with a five minute session per day. After a while, you'll increase this time automatically, as you experience the benefits of meditation and you'll want to meditate more often.

5. Setting aside the same time every day for your meditation is a good idea – it gets you into a routine that you can look forward to. Some people find that the best time for meditation is in the morning before you begin your daily work, while others find that the evening is more enjoyable, after you have taken your bath and washed away the stress of the work day. Whatever your preference, make it your routine, your sanctuary where you go to find yourself.

I find time during my work day to meditate for a few minutes in addition to my nightly meditation at home. I close my office door, take the phone off the hook, tune into spiritual new age music on my computer (courtesy of Sirius satellite music) and spend a few minutes refreshing my mind and soul.

As I indicated before, music greatly enhances your meditative experience. In addition to gentle music, there are a great number of guided meditation CDs available, that lead you through the relaxation and meditation process. You can download many of them for free.

No matter which method you use to mediate, the ultimate purpose of meditation is to calm your mind and to experience inner peace and happiness. When you practice meditation on a regular basis, you will easily reach the intuitive stage of your mind where thoughts vanish and your subconscious mind becomes accessible to you. It is there where you find your inner peace, your intuition, your spirituality, and your sacred self.

Appendices

Appendix C

CREATIVE VISUALIZATION TECHNIQUES

As we have seen in Chapter 5, visualization is just another term for imagination. Every child knows how to do this instinctively – just as adults we tend to forget how to use our imagination to our benefits. So, I am going to prompt your memory and inspire you to imagine with me, as we discuss some of the areas in life almost everyone wants to improve on: managing your day, losing weight, healing, relationships and love, material possessions, having a great job and great wealth.

Sometimes visualization may sound a lot like meditation, but there's at least one critical difference. Meditation often involves getting still and clearing your mind. In visualization, instead of clearing your mind, you become laser-focused on your goals and dreams. You create a vision and then gradually and methodically clarify it down to the most minute detail.

Managing Your Day

Let's say, you are a "Soccer Mom" and you wake up this morning feeling totally overwhelmed with all the things you have to do today, from getting the kids up, making their breakfast and getting them to eat it, to driving them to school, making the beds and cleaning the house while they are away, washing the dirty soccer clothes so they'll be ready for the next game, making lunch, picking the kids up again from school, feeding them, helping them with their homework, picking them up again for soccer practice, taking your girl to dance class while the boys practice soccer, going food shopping for dinner tonight, picking up all the kids, taking another kid back home because his parents asked you to help out, getting the kids to wash up, making dinner, taking a quick shower and greeting your hubby with a big smile and a kiss when he gets home from work... Wow, I'm dizzy myself just writing about these tasks and I can imagine how you feel having to do them all!

So, let's visualize your way through this day and see how this helps.

> First of all, you have already begun to visualize by thinking about all the tasks that are ahead of you today. You already have a clear picture in your mind what has to be done when and in what order. Now use the power of your imagination to see yourself performing all these tasks in an organized, simple and effective manner without difficulty or stress.

> Visualize your darling children waking up with a good disposition, which you support further by hugging them with a warm wakeup kiss that makes them feel secure and happy. See your happy children dress themselves this morning, leaving you ample time to make their breakfast. Imagine yourself preparing a simple yet nutritious breakfast that your children like and rewarding them with another hug and affirmation that you love them. See in your mind how everyone is off to a good start today.

> As you are driving them to work, visualize how you will tackle the numerous tasks at home that await you when you get back. Plan them in every detail, see yourself economizing on time wherever possible, such as putting the clothes in the wash machine first and defrosting the lunch meat while making the beds and cleaning the house. In your imagination, give yourself set amounts of time for each task – see the clock on the wall and perform by it.

> When you visualize in such detail you will find that you have ample time to accomplish every task when you actually do them – with time left over to take a rest and spend some on yourself. Your entire day will be a breeze to get through and you will be happy and content with your family at the end of the day, just as you have imagined it!

Losing Weight

Oh, those extra pounds- don't we all want to get rid of them and have a wonderful, proportionate, healthy body that is admired by others? You can achieve this body by creative visualization.

➤ Instead of looking in the mirror, look into your imaginary mirror, the one that is always available, the one that will reflect back to you the body you seek. Look into this mirror often, mornings and night and several times of the day. Close your eyes and admire yourself in this mirror, let your eyes caress the slender shape of your hips, your small waist and your shapely legs. If you're a guy, admire your broad shoulders, big biceps and washboard abs.

➤ You know that exercise helps you achieve this great body. So see yourself at the gym working out with friends, enjoying the new sensations of your body as it develops strong muscles and increases its flexibility and stamina. If you prefer to do a different type of exercise, such as dancing, swimming, hiking, biking or horseback riding, imagine yourself doing these activities with great joy and excitement.

➤ You also know that food is the fuel for your muscles. So you visualize yourself feeding those muscles with nutritious food that is tasty and satisfying. See in your mind's eye how this good food strengthens your body and gives you the energy you need to enjoy your life to the fullest. Never, ever think about food as being bad for you and making you fat.

➤ Visualize your family, friends and co-workers compliment you on your body. See the admiring and jealous glances from them and others you meet casually. See yourself showing off your body on the beach or at the pool in your bathing suit and love every minute of it.

➤ Imagine yourself wearing your "skinny" clothes, the ones you love so much but could not get into for a long time.

Visualize yourself buying new clothes in your perfect size, now that you can wear fashionable clothes again. See yourself being the center of attention and admiration at a social function, or perhaps at a high school or college reunion.

When you visualize yourself like this your subconscious mind "sees" your body like this also and directs the rest of your being to do all the things necessary to bring it into reality. This means that you will "automatically" start to eat the right foods, eat less of them, and exercise more to achieve the desired results. You already know that how you think affects your body – so think "slim" and soon you will be slim.

Healing

When you use visualization techniques to heal yourself it helps if you know a bit about how the body's immune system works. This system is designed to guard you against viruses, toxins, and millions of bacteria and microbes that invade your body. It blocks these intruders before they can get in.

Without getting too technical, let's just confirm here that the immune system has major components, one of which is the white blood cells. These cells have the job to identify foreign bodies, to "gobble them up" and carry them away and out of the body. So, when you are sick – let's assume you have the flu – you might begin your visualization by imagining one of these white blood cells swimming in your blood stream like a shark on the lookout for its prey – the flu virus.

> ➤ Watch this hunt and kill in your mind's eye as if you saw it on television: the white blood cells seek and find the flu virus; it swims near it and, since it is much larger than the virus, simply squashes it with its own bulk.

> ➤ If there are multiple flu virus organisms, the white cells call for reinforcements and a huge army of cells arrive to crush the invaders. Imagine this battle over and over again with the white blood cells emerging always as the winner.

Other methods of visualizing for self-healing are to

➤ Visualize clear, pure energy entering your body from above and filling your entire body. In this method, the objective is not to kill intruders one by one but to create a body environment where intruders have no place. When the energy enters your body the intruders simply vanish into thin air. Imagine little puffs of smoke as they disintegrate – with every puff your body becomes purer and healthier.

➤ Imagine a river of pure water rushing through your body carrying away all disease and impurity.

➤ Imagine your happiness hormones, your endorphins, march like a huge army to the sound of your laughter and defeat all intruders. So laugh a lot to keep these powerful hormones engaged all the time!

➤ Use the power of your own imagination to come up with methods that suit you in your fight against illness and disease. When you have visualized the destruction and defeat of your illness, imagine yourself as completely healed. Feel your strength, enjoy your health and live your life to the fullest!

Material Possessions

Manifesting a material thing into your life, like a new computer, or your dream house, is the easiest form of visualization. Depending on the item you wish for, it may take a little or longer time for this item to manifest in your life. If you have any doubt about your ability to visualize and thus manifest your desires into your life, start with a simple thing. For example, visualize an automatic espresso machine, the kind you have seen on television recently or the one your friend has shown you the other day.

➤ Find a picture of this espresso machine in a magazine or get it online or directly from the manufacturer. Cut this picture out and put it on your vision board, or, if your vision board is posted at home, put it on your desk in the office or stick it on your computer, somewhere you'll see it every day, all day long.

➤ Every time you look at this picture, imagine yourself making this espresso. See yourself putting the coffee into the machine, placing a small cup beneath the pour spout and pressing the brew button. Hear the hissing sound of the steam as the machine brews the espresso. See the black coffee dribble into the cup.

➤ In your imagination, smell the wonderful aroma of the espresso and taste the coffee. Enjoy its robust flavor and savor the coffee in your mouth for a second before swallowing it. Feel the hot liquid go down your throat warming you up and giving you a soothing and relaxing sensation. Know that you own this espresso machine and that you can have this great coffee anytime you desire.

➤ Visualize a package arriving at your door. See yourself looking at the sender and knowing that it's your espresso machine. See yourself unwrapping the parcel and taking the machine out of its packaging. Imagine washing the washable parts, filling the reservoir with water and plugging it into the electric outlet. Imagine making the first cup of coffee and offering it to your spouse, who loves the excellent brew as much as you do.

➤ Repeat this visualization every day, several times of the day and never waiver in your belief that you already have this espresso machine. See it sitting on your kitchen counter, in exactly the size and color you want, and soon it really will be there! Not through hocus-pocus... but through the vibrational pull of your thoughts that compell others who feel them to act. Someone might gift you this espresso machine, or you might purchase it yourself with money that just showed up. Believe it, and it will happen!

Relationships and Love

Let's say you have been dreaming of your perfect mate, your partner for life, who will love you always and be there for you no matter what. You don't know what he/she looks like, but you know his essence and that he will make you happy for the rest of your life. You want to bring this person into your life – now.

When you visualize a material thing, like the espresso machine above or a car for example, you imagine it through your five senses. You see this car in full color, you hear its engine roar as you speed up from zero to 60 mph in six seconds in your imagination; you smell the new leather and you feel the firmness and cushioning of the seats when you touch them. And, if you are really into this car you might even find a way to taste it...

Well, with people it is the same way. Use your five senses to get to know this person that you want to attract into your life, and know for sure that this person actually exists. See him/her in your mind's eye and then begin to describe him, as if you were telling your best friend about this perfect human being you have just met:

> ➤ Tell her how he looks, height, weight, body shape, hair color, eye color, facial features and his hands. Does he resemble a well known movie star or does he have star quality all by himself?

> ➤ Describe his voice, and the tone in which he speaks with you; see his smile and describe how it makes you feel when you are with him. Smell the fragrance of his after shave; feel the touch of his skin and explore his kiss.

> ➤ How does he walk? Does he have lots of energy or is he more laid back? See him beside you as you are engaged in your own favorite activities and feel how he complements you in every way.

> ➤ Imagine the two of you a few years in the future when you have a family already. Visualize your life together and know how perfect it is.

Do not for a moment think that you are just day dreaming. Day dreaming is just a way to pass idle time. When you visualize like this however, you have a purpose in mind – you are attracting your perfect partner into your life. Your visions of him are thought patterns, and as you already know, thought is energy that travels like a radio beam in all directions. Your visualization thought has a certain frequency and your perfect partner is the only one who can receive your thought energy on this frequency. Believe – and he will show up in your life!

A Great Job

If you want to have a new and exciting job, you need to prepare a little before visualizing yourself in it. It helps if you know what kind of job you are looking for – an office job, a lawn care job, a job in an ice cream parlor? Do you just want a promotion to a job someone else is holding at the moment, or do you want to move across the country to take on a completely new challenge?

If you begin to visualize "an outdoor job" without specifying exactly what you mean by that, you might end up getting your wish by being offered a sanitation associate job with a local trash collection firm, whereas you had a forest ranger job in mind. So be specific in what you want before you start to visualize.

For our example here, let's assume you are currently working part time for McDonalds making hamburgers while finishing your college degree and you want a job as an accounting clerk in a big firm, and you are now qualified for the position you are seeking.

> ➤ Begin by visualizing your morning routine as you are getting ready for your new job. After you have taken your refreshing shower, decide on the clothes you will be wearing today. Imagine selecting the new office attire which you purchased recently and only slightly glancing at the jeans and tee-shirts that used to be your daily uniform. See yourself dressing for success!

➤ Visualize yourself arriving at your new job, greeting your office co-workers and being greeted by them. Imagine your office cubicle or desk where you are working now. See it in all details, the computer, the adding machine, the telephone, the business card holder with your new business card, and your office chair. Feel how comfortable it is and how it supports your back.

➤ Hear the phone ring and see yourself picking it up and introducing yourself as the new hire in this office. Feel proud of your competence when you accurately answer the caller's questions. Know that this job is yours already and that you are perfect for it.

➤ Visualize your first performance evaluation at this job. Hear your boss singing your praises and telling you how glad he is having hired you.

➤ Now, having firmly established in your mind's eye that this is the job you desire and that you are happy and content in it, step back a bit in time and see yourself at your first job interview with this firm. Imagine stepping off the elevator and going confidently into the reception area to meet your new boss. See how easily you interact with each other, how quickly you grasp the duties and responsibilities of your new job and how certain you are about your abilities to meet them all. See yourself leaving this interview with the certainty that the job is yours.

➤ Lastly, take one more step backwards and see yourself preparing your resume and filling out the job application. See how easily your pen glides over the paper, giving the best possible answers to the questions asked and how your confidence and self assuredness can be easily read between the lines.

Now that you have gone over these easy steps in your mind and have repeated these visualizations numerous times, you are ready to take the step for real. Send out the applications to your preferred employers and your dream job will be yours in no time at all!

Money

Say, you want to take your family on a fabulous vacation to Disney World (the kids have been bugging you about this for months now and you sort of promised) but you have no money. You figure you'll need about $5,000 for your family of four, for the airfares, hotel for a week, car rental, food and of course, the amusement park tickets and souvenirs. What to do? Well, start visualizing!

➤ Imagine a check – you know how to do this because you've seen plenty of them in your lifetime. Imagine this check having your name written on it and today's date – but you can't see the bank it's drawn on, nor the person whose signature is on it. See yourself holding this check in your hands, jumping up and down for joy that you now have the needed funds. See yourself running to your spouse, hugging him/her waiving the check and feel the happiness you both experience now. Believe that this has happened already now, and have faith in your beliefs.

➤ Imagine yourself writing the deposit slip, endorsing the check, entering the amount in your checkbook or electronic accounts, and taking the check to the bank. See yourself smiling at the bank teller and saying that this money is for your long deserved vacation. See yourself planning your trip, checking on flight reservations and hotels and imagine your conversation with your children when you tell them that you'll be going to see The Mouse very soon!

➤ Repeat this visualization exercise every day, in fact, every time you think about it. Repeat it in every detail, see the money in your bank account, see the smiles on your children's faces, feel the happiness in your soul and do not waver in your belief that it has already happened!

Your money will arrive in time for your vacation. It may come from various sources, an unexpected bonus at work, a gift from a relative, a dividend on stocks you own but have forgotten about, from the sale of an item in your garage that your neighbor wants all of a sudden or from other sources. Results may come immediately all at once, or in stages over time, and it will be enough for your vacation!

Great Wealth

First, you must know what great wealth means to you. Is the wealth you seek monetary wealth or spiritual wealth? Do you want wealth in your relationships, in love, in health? You can see how relevant this question is.

Let us assume you want material wealth, which you define as living in a million dollar mansion, having a 60 foot ocean going yacht, your own corporate jet and $20 million in the bank and portfolio investments.

Visualizing this great wealth differs only slightly from manifesting money. After all, you could visualize receiving $5,000 per day, and soon you would be very wealthy. However, great wealth is easier manifested if you imagine yourself owning and growing a business.

But first, let me reiterate – you must never see yourself as needing or wanting money and great wealth. Instead you must always imagine yourself as already having it. This cannot be over-emphasized enough. When you want something and constantly keep this feeling and desire in your mind, your subconscious mind considers this as your greatest desire, and keeps you in this constantly wanting something and never having it.

Begin your visualization process by focusing on the mindset you need to have to be successful in business:

> ➤ Know that you are resourceful, powerful, imaginative, well educated, self assured, trustworthy, and a person of highest integrity and excellent business sense. Know that you are a money magnet and that wealth comes to you easily.

> ➤ If you already know what kind of business you would like to have, visualize yourself running this business. If

you do not know it yet, that does not matter – you can still see yourself in your executive suite on the top floor of a luxurious office building overlooking the city below you. Imagine every detail of your office; see your office staff coming in to get your instructions; imagine yourself at the head of the board room conference table making policy decisions concerning your business.

➤ Visualize the daily, weekly, monthly and annual profit reports presented to you by your staff. See the income and profit figures rising every period. See yourself rewarding your key personnel with bonuses for a job well done.

➤ Visualize the checks coming in every day from your customers. Visualize the daily orders doubling and quadrupling monthly. See your company's product becoming a best seller in your industry. See your name on the front cover of your industry's leading publication followed by a highly complimentary article about your business.

➤ Imagine receiving top honors from highly regarded organizations in your area, and being the talk of the town.

➤ And lastly, see yourself living the kind of life you consider a life of great wealth. If this includes your private jet, see yourself flying in it to business meetings across the country or taking your family to Florida to go on a deep sea fishing trip. If it includes a chauffeur driven limousine, by all means, see yourself lounging in it sipping a glass of champagne. Let your imagination take you wherever you desire – it is your visualization and your life that you are manifesting through it.

A final word on visualization: when you visualize your results they are most likely going to come in a natural and gradual manner with one step leading to another. Most likely your results will be based on some event or connection from your past. Do not expect lottery winnings or windfall payments although these are also possibilities and have indeed happened to many who routinely and confidently visualize their dreams.

On two occasions I personally received $20,000 payments "out of the blue" when I visualized receiving money without knowing where it would come from: the first time when a contract for the purchase of real estate was cancelled by the developer and I got my down payment back after two years. I never expected to get any money back and had thought instead that I would have to go through with the construction of the house that I no longer wanted. The second time happened just recently, when a note was paid off by someone who owed me money. I had thought that this note was uncollectible and had already forgotten about it.

Lastly, let us not forget that your visualizations and manifestations will be most effective if you are grateful for what you have already received. The law of attraction states that what you put out to the universe you will receive back multiplied. A statement of gratitude sends out a very powerful message to the universe and the universe reacts by making your visualizations reality in your life.

The law of attraction is always working for you and everyone else – there is no exception to this rule. Know this and apply your newfound knowledge to your life and you will achieve everything you have always wished for.

Appendix D

HOW TO CREATE EFFECTIVE AFFIRMATIONS

Rules for effective affirmations:

1. Say only positive words: use short, carefully construct-ed positive words or phrases and repeat them as often as possible to be effective.

2. Always speak in the present tense, never in the future: you must be positive and phrase your affirmation in the present tense – "I am worthy", not "I will be worthy". If you speak in future terms, your subconscious mind will take it for granted that you "will be worthy in the future" and will grant you your wish – in the future, and never now.

3. Be relaxed: saying your affirmations while clenching your teeth is not going to bring good results. Try to be relaxed, joyful, feeling abundant and happy when repeat-ing your affirmations.

4. Concentrate on what you are saying: just repeating your affirmations without giving any thought to them will also not yield the desired results. Try to concentrate on every word, pronouncing it clearly and with conviction.

5. Repeat your affirmations often: you should say your affirmations at least once a day; say them in the morning when you get up and say them again at night just before you go to bed. Say them in the shower – even better, sing them in the shower and while you do your house work or drive to the grocery store. Repetition is the key to effec-tive affirmations.

6. Believe that what you are affirming is already fact: this is the clincher – you must believe deep down in your soul that what you are affirming is in fact true. Do not allow any doubt to enter your mind. If you feel an insecurity creeping into your mind, brush it off immediately, and repeat your affirmation again, this time with full conviction and in a loud voice. By doing so you will tell your subconscious that you mean business!

7. Say your affirmations with passion: it is a good idea to muster up as much passion as you can when you say your affirmations. Put your heart and soul into the words as you are speaking them and the impact on your subconscious mind will be twice as strong.

8. Write down your affirmations: this is a great way of keeping them in your mind all the time. Put them up on post-it notes, stick them on your refrigerator, on the bathroom mirror, keep them in your wallet, hang them on your key chain – and repeat them to yourself as often as you can!

9. For greater impact, look in the mirror when you are saying your affirmations: When you speak with another person, you look them into the eyes to truly connect with them. So do this also when you are speaking with yourself, with your subconscious, and you will magnify the importance of the message to yourself.

Affirmations for Self Esteem

I am worthy

I believe in myself

I am whole

I am perfect

I am creative

I am wonderful

I feel good

I think positively

I have balance in my life

I am capable

I can accomplish anything I set my mind to

I make excellent choices

I am strong and powerful

I am abundant

I have unlimited potential

I am successful

Affirmations for Health, Mind and Body

I am relaxed

I feel comfortable

I feel at peace

I feel good

I am calm and relaxed

I love myself and my body

My mind is calm and serene

I have great health

I am full of energy and vitality

I have self confidence

I think positive thoughts

I heal quickly and easily
I am happy
I am safe
I am free
I enjoy life
I am special
I am beautiful just the way I am
I am blessed
My mind is focused
I control my thoughts

Affirmations for Love

I love myself
I honor myself
I attract wonderful relationships
I choose healthy relationships
I am at peace
I am open to love
I allow love to find me
I trust in love
I deserve love
I enjoy harmonious relationships
My life is full of joy
I love my partner
I am surrounded by love
I love my life
I radiate love and happiness
I am happy and fulfilled

Affirmations for Wealth

I am successful

I am wealthy and financially free

Money flows to me easily

I am a money magnet

I have incredible energy

Challenges help me grow

I can accomplish anything

I am powerful and successful

I am strong and powerful

I can handle anything

I have all the money I need

I am bold and confident

I am good enough

I am worthy of great wealth

Affirmations for Happiness

I am at peace

I am relaxed and happy

I enjoy my life

I attract abundance

I attract good friends

I have a strong and healthy body

I am fun to be with

I am grateful for my God given gifts

I am blessed

I am happy

I deserve good things in life

I deserve to be loved

Acknowledgements

It has been said that when the student is ready, the teacher will appear. I am deeply indebted to the teachers who have come into my life during the past two years and who have opened my eyes and mind to the powers within.

My gratitude goes to my mentors:

Jase Souder, who showed me the connection between the mind and the heart and who never gave up on me no matter how resistant I was to learning new concepts; many of the concepts discussed here were first brought to my attention by Jase in his seminar so aptly named The Bridge;

Harold Maloy, who took me to the top of a mountain to rediscover nature, and who showed me how to feel the universal God love and summon it whenever needed;

Glenn Dietzel, who inspired me to write this book and whose staff at http://www.AwakenTheAuthorWithin.com gave invaluable assistance during the writing and compilation of it;

...and the many writers, who through their writings or voice recordings have motivated me to explore my mind and grow emotionally and spiritually: Michael J. Losier, Rhonda Byrne, Jack Canfield, Marci Shimoff, Janet and Chris Attwood, Joe Vitale, James Arthur Ray, Wallace D. Wattles, Louise Hay, Esther Hicks, Charles F. Haanel, Robert Collier, Deepak Chopra, Dr. Wayne W. Dyer, Mark Victor Hansen, and T. Harv Eker, just to mention a few;

...and to my dear friends Olga and Joe Rickards, who helped me conceptualize this book and who encouraged me with their enthusiasm and support throughout the writing and editing process.

I thank my family, who still love me in spite of all my imperfections, and the numerous named and unnamed contributors to these pages who shared their experiences with me so I could pass them on to you for your understanding and learning.

About the Author

Andrea Lucas was born and raised in Vienna, Austria. Early on her dream was to see the world and to experience life to the fullest. So, barely 18 years old, she left Austria and headed for Canada where she started her career as a finance professional.

Over the next two decades Andrea earned several degrees, moved to Puerto Rico and then to Washington, DC, where she became a Director of the World Bank. A decade later, Andrea started her own company overseas and built an organization that provided expertise in infrastructure and industrial project development to the governments of dozens of developing nations and to numerous private industrial enterprises.

After returning to the US, Andrea enjoyed a period of semi-retirement, interrupted only by occasional personal development seminars. It was at one these seminars that a life-altering event occurred that changed her focus from being a business-woman to being a mentor, author and successful communicator.

The discovery of her "Script" (the blueprint of how she was to live her life that was formed when she was just a little girl), had a profound impact on her. She felt compelled to write the book, "My Life's A Mess – But I Can Fix It!" and to share her experiences with others in the hope that they could be spared the disappointment, frustration and lack of fulfillment she had felt all of her life in spite of her professional accomplishments.

4110722

Made in the USA
Charleston, SC
01 December 2009